NEW YORK NIGHTLIFE GUIDE 2016

RESTAURANTS, BARS, LOUNGES & CLUBS

The Most Positively Reviewed and Recommended Places by Visitors

NEW YORK NIGHTLIFE GUIDE 2016
Best Rated Nightlife Spots in New York City, NY

© Andrew F. McNaught, 2016
© E.G.P. Editorial, 2016

Printed in USA.

ISBN-13: 978-1518637049
ISBN-10: 1518637043

Copyright © 2016
All rights reserved.

NEW YORK NIGHTLIFE GUIDE 2016
Most Recommended Nightlife Spots in New York

This directory is dedicated to New York City Business Owners and Managers
who provide the experience that the locals and tourists enjoy.
Thanks you very much for all that you do and thank for being the "People Choice".

Thanks to everyone that posts their reviews online and
the amazing reviews sites that make our life easier.

The places listed in this book are the most positively reviewed
and recommended by locals and travelers from around the world.

Thank you for your time and enjoy the directory that is
designed with locals and tourist in mind!

TOP 500
NIGHTLIFE SPOTS
The Most Recommended
(from #1 to #500)

well - its a bit short on detail - we guess they were too pissed to write a lenghty reviews! Have fun exploring these places

love Maria, Jo Stretz e Jane
xxx

#1
Stage Karaoke & Lounge
Cuisines: Karaoke, Lounge
Average price: Modest
Area: Midtown West, Koreatown
Address: 23 W 32nd St
New York, NY 10001
Phone: (212) 629-4141

#2
Parlay Cafe
Cuisines: Hookah Bar
Average price: Modest
Area: Harlem
Address: 1780 Amsterdam Ave
New York, NY 10031
Phone: (646) 823-9880

#3
Mosaic Cafe & Lounge
Cuisines: Wine Bar, Lounge, Venues, Event Space
Average price: Modest
Area: Astoria
Address: 25-19 24th Ave
Astoria, NY 11102
Phone: (718) 728-0708

#4
Pocket Bar NYC
Cuisines: Wine Bar
Average price: Modest
Area: Hell's Kitchen, Midtown West
Address: 455 W 48th St
New York, NY 10036
Phone: (646) 682-9062

#5
Delia's Lounge & Restaurant
Cuisines: Lounge, Wine Bar, Seafood
Average price: Modest
Area: Fort Hamilton, Bay Ridge
Address: 9224 3rd Ave
Brooklyn, NY 11209
Phone: (718) 745-7999

#6
Featherweight
Cuisines: Bar
Average price: Modest
Area: East Williamsburg
Address: 135 Graham Ave
Brooklyn, NY 11206
Phone: (202) 907-3372

#7
Twenty3 Supper Club
Cuisines: American, Lounge
Average price: Expensive
Area: Fort Hamilton, Bay Ridge
Address: 8915 5th Ave
Brooklyn, NY 11209
Phone: (718) 921-2323

#8
Iron Horse NYC
Cuisines: Dive Bar, Pub
Average price: Inexpensive
Area: Financial District
Address: 32 Cliff St
New York, NY 10038
Phone: (646) 546-5426

#9
Babel NYC
Cuisines: Lounge, Hookah Bar, Night Club
Average price: Modest
Area: East Village, Alphabet City
Address: 129 Ave C
New York, NY 10009
Phone: (212) 505-3468

#10
The Ship
Cuisines: Cocktail Bar
Average price: Modest
Area: SoHo
Address: 158 Lafayette St
New York, NY 10013
Phone: (212) 219-8496

#11
La Nuit
Cuisines: Mediterranean, Tapas Bar, Hookah Bar
Average price: Modest
Area: Upper East Side
Address: 1134 1st Ave
New York, NY 10065
Phone: (646) 454-0499

#12
Dead Drop
Cuisines: Cocktail Bar
Average price: Modest
Area: East Village
Address: 166 1st Ave
New York, NY 10009
Phone: (212) 777-1552

#13
Full Cup
Cuisines: Bar
Average price: Inexpensive
Area: Stapleton
Address: 388 Van Duzer St
Staten Island, NY 10304
Phone: (718) 442-4224

#14
Cloud Social Rooftop Bar
Cuisines: Cocktail Bar
Average price: Modest
Area: Midtown West, Koreatown
Address: 6 W 32 St, 17th Fl
New York, NY 10001
Phone: (212) 904-1092

#15
Tantra Lounge
Cuisines: Lounge, Hookah Bar
Average price: Modest
Area: Astoria
Address: 35-50 31 St
Astoria, NY 11106
Phone: (718) 937-4574

#16
Blackbird
Cuisines: Bar
Average price: Modest
Area: East Village, Alphabet City
Address: 162 Ave B
New York, NY 10009
Phone: (646) 807-3754

#17
Old Man Hustle
Cuisines: Cocktail Bar, Dive Bar, Comedy Club
Average price: Inexpensive
Area: Lower East Side
Address: 39 Essex St
New York, NY 10002
Phone: (212) 253-7747

#18
Camp David NYC
Cuisines: Tapas, Lounge
Average price: Modest
Area: East Village, Alphabet City
Address: 221 Ave B
New York, NY 10009
Phone: (212) 228-0170

#19
MikNic Lounge
Cuisines: Lounge
Average price: Inexpensive
Area: Columbia Street Waterfront District
Address: 200 Columbia St
Brooklyn, NY 11231
Phone: (917) 770-1984

#20
The Social Butterfly
Cuisines: Lounge, Night Club
Average price: Modest
Area: Prospect Heights, Clinton Hill
Address: 857 Atlantic Ave
Brooklyn, NY 11238
Phone: (347) 799-2064

#21
Lot45
Cuisines: Lounge, Cocktail Bar
Average price: Modest
Area: Bushwick
Address: 411 Troutman St
Brooklyn, NY 11237
Phone: (347) 505-9155

#22
Randolph Brooklyn
Cuisines: Cocktail Bar, American, Breakfast & Brunch
Average price: Modest
Area: Williamsburg - South Side
Address: 104 S 4th St
Brooklyn, NY 11249
Phone: (646) 383-3623

#23
The Roof
Cuisines: Cocktail Bar, Lounge
Average price: Expensive
Area: Midtown West
Address: 124 W 57th St, 29th Fl
Manhattan, NY 10019
Phone: (212) 707-8008

#24
Manhattan Cricket Club
Cuisines: Cocktail Bar
Average price: Expensive
Area: Upper West Side
Address: 226 W 79th St
New York, NY 10024
Phone: (646) 823-9252

#25
Gottscheer Hall
Cuisines: Caterer, German, Pub
Average price: Inexpensive
Area: Ridgewood
Address: 657 Fairview Ave
Ridgewood, NY 11385
Phone: (718) 366-3030

#26
205 Club
Cuisines: Lounge
Average price: Modest
Area: Lower East Side
Address: 205 Chrystie St
New York, NY 10002
Phone: (917) 583-5790

#27
bibi
Cuisines: Wine Bar
Average price: Modest
Area: East Village, Alphabet City
Address: 211 E 4th St
New York, NY 10009
Phone: (212) 673-2424

#28
Brooklyn Terrace
Cuisines: Lounge
Average price: Modest
Area: Downtown Brooklyn
Address: 216-228 Duffield St
Brooklyn, NY 11201
Phone: (347) 390-1891

#29
Doris
Cuisines: Bar
Average price: Modest
Area: Bedford Stuyvesant, Clinton Hill
Address: 1088 Fulton St
Brooklyn, NY 11238
Phone: (347) 240-3350

#30
Time Out New York Lounge
Cuisines: Lounge
Average price: Modest
Area: Hell's Kitchen, Midtown West
Address: 340 W 50th St
Manhattan, NY 10019
Phone: (646) 871-1730

#31
706
Cuisines: Dive Bar, Sports Bar
Average price: Inexpensive
Area: Prospect Heights
Address: 706 Washington Ave
Brooklyn, NY 11238
Phone: (646) 456-8444

#33
Destination Bar & Grill
Cuisines: American, Cocktail Bar
Average price: Inexpensive
Area: East Village, Alphabet City
Address: 211 Ave A
New York, NY 10009
Phone: (212) 388-9844

#32
Analogue
Cuisines: Cocktail Bar, Jazz, Blues, Lounge
Average price: Expensive
Area: Greenwich Village
Address: 19 W 8th St
New York, NY 10011
Phone: (212) 432-0200

#34
TBA Brooklyn
Cuisines: Bar, Night Club
Average price: Modest
Area: Williamsburg - South Side, South Williamsburg
Address: 395 Wythe Ave
New York, NY 11249
Phone: (347) 529-4429

#35
Beloved
Cuisines: Cocktail Bar
Average price: Modest
Area: Greenpoint
Address: 674 Manhattan Ave
Brooklyn, NY 11222
Phone: (347) 457-5448

#36
The Brewery
Cuisines: Sports Bar
Average price: Modest
Area: Astoria
Address: 49-18 30th Ave
Woodside, NY 11377
Phone: (718) 777-8007

#37
Subject
Cuisines: Cocktail Bar
Average price: Modest
Area: Lower East Side
Address: 188 Suffolk St
New York, NY 10002
Phone: (646) 422-7898

#38
The NoMad Bar
Cuisines: Cocktail Bar
Average price: Expensive
Area: Flatiron
Address: 10 W 28th St
New York, NY 10001
Phone: (212) 796-1500

#39
Clockwork Bar
Cuisines: Dive Bar
Average price: Inexpensive
Area: Chinatown, Lower East Side
Address: 21 Essex St
New York, NY 10002
Phone: (212) 677-4545

#40
Covenhoven
Cuisines: Bar
Average price: Inexpensive
Area: Crown Heights
Address: 730 Classon Ave
Brooklyn, NY 11238
Phone: (718) 483-9950

#41
The Harp
Cuisines: Pub, Sports Bar
Average price: Inexpensive
Area: Bay Ridge
Address: 7710 3rd Ave
Brooklyn, NY 11209
Phone: (718) 745-4277

#42
Nitecap
Cuisines: Cocktail Bar
Average price: Modest
Area: Lower East Side
Address: 120 Rivington St
New York, NY 10002
Phone: (212) 466-3361

#43
Bonnie Vee
Cuisines: Cocktail Bar
Average price: Modest
Area: Lower East Side
Address: 17 Stanton St
New York, NY 10002
Phone: (917) 639-3352

#44
The Sampler Bushwick
Cuisines: Bar
Average price: Modest
Area: Bushwick
Address: 234 Starr St
Brooklyn, NY 11237
Phone: (718) 484-3560

#45
Kion Ceviche Bar
Cuisines: Cocktail Bar, Latin American, Peruvian
Average price: Modest
Area: Williamsburg - North Side
Address: 568 Union Ave
Brooklyn, NY 11211
Phone: (718) 302-5680

#46
Mama's Bar
Cuisines: Dive Bar, Sports Bar
Average price: Inexpensive
Area: East Village, Alphabet City
Address: 34 Ave B
New York, NY 10009
Phone: (212) 777-5729

#47
Red Hook Bait & Tackle
Cuisines: Dive Bar
Average price: Inexpensive
Area: Red Hook
Address: 320 Van Brunt St
Brooklyn, NY 11231
Phone: (718) 451-4665

#48
Beso Lounge
Cuisines: Lounge
Average price: Modest
Area: Norwood
Address: 320 E 204th St
Bronx, NY 10467
Phone: (646) 807-4522

#49
Juke Bar
Cuisines: Bar
Average price: Modest
Area: East Village
Address: 196 2nd Ave
New York, NY 10003
Phone: (212) 228-7464

#50
Mundo
Cuisines: Bar, Mediterranean, Music Venues
Average price: Expensive
Area: Astoria, Long Island City
Address: 37-06 36th St
Long Island City, NY 11101
Phone: (718) 706-8636

#51
Cherry Tree
Cuisines: Bar
Average price: Inexpensive
Area: Park Slope, Gowanus
Address: 65 4th Ave
Brooklyn, NY 11217
Phone: (718) 399-1353

#52
Don't Tell Mama
Cuisines: Bar, American, Cabaret
Average price: Modest
Area: Hell's Kitchen, Midtown West, Theater District
Address: 343 W 46th St
New York, NY 10036
Phone: (212) 757-0788

#53
Splitty
Cuisines: Bar, Breakfast & Brunch
Average price: Inexpensive
Area: Clinton Hill
Address: 415 Myrtle Ave
Brooklyn, NY 11205
Phone: (718) 643-2867

#54
Bar 718
Cuisines: Bar
Average price: Inexpensive
Area: South Slope
Address: 718 5th Ave
Brooklyn, NY 11232
Phone: (718) 499-2661

#55
Lamoza
Cuisines: Middle Eastern, Hookah Bar
Average price: Modest
Area: Bay Ridge
Address: 7704 3rd Ave
Brooklyn, NY 11209
Phone: (718) 238-3625

#56
The Village Underground
Cuisines: Night Club, Lounge
Average price: Modest
Area: Greenwich Village
Address: 130 W 3rd St
New York, NY 10012
Phone: (212) 777-7745

#57
E's Bar
Cuisines: Bar
Average price: Modest
Area: Upper West Side
Address: 511 Amsterdam Ave
New York, NY 10033
Phone: (212) 877-0961

#58
Botanic Lab
Cuisines: Cocktail Bar
Average price: Expensive
Area: Lower East Side
Address: 86 Orchard St
New York, NY 10002
Phone: (212) 777-2664

#59
The Monro Pub
Cuisines: Pub
Average price: Inexpensive
Area: South Slope, Park Slope
Address: 481 5th Ave
Brooklyn, NY 11215
Phone: (718) 499-2005

#60
The Shanty
Cuisines: Bar
Average price: Modest
Area: Williamsburg - North Side
Address: 79 Richardson St
Brooklyn, NY 11211
Phone: (718) 412-0874

#61
Karaoke Shout - Astoria
Cuisines: Karaoke, Bar
Average price: Modest
Area: Astoria
Address: 32-46 Steinway St
Astoria, NY 11103
Phone: (718) 569-0080

#62
Wine and Roses
Cuisines: Wine Bar
Average price: Modest
Area: Upper West Side
Address: 286 Columbus Ave
New York, NY 10023
Phone: (212) 579-9463

#63
Bar Thalia
Cuisines: Lounge, Wine Bar
Average price: Modest
Area: Upper West Side
Address: 2537 Broadway
New York, NY 10025
Phone: (646) 597-7340

#64
The Mayflower
Cuisines: Lounge
Average price: Modest
Area: Clinton Hill
Address: 132 Greene Ave
Brooklyn, NY 11238
Phone: (718) 576-3584

#65
Glorietta Baldy
Cuisines: Bar
Average price: Modest
Area: Bedford Stuyvesant, Clinton Hill
Address: 502 Franklin Ave
Brooklyn, NY 11238
Phone: (347) 529-1944

#66
Hollow Nickel
Cuisines: Pub, American
Average price: Modest
Area: Boerum Hill
Address: 494 Atlantic Ave
New York, NY 11217
Phone: (347) 236-3417

#67
Vino Levantino
Cuisines: Wine Bar, Middle Eastern
Average price: Modest
Area: Upper West Side
Address: 210 W 94th St
New York, NY 10025
Phone: (212) 280-3333

#68
Terraza 7
Cuisines: Bar, Music Venues, Jazz, Blues
Average price: Modest
Area: Elmhurst
Address: 40-19 Gleane St
Elmhurst, NY 11373
Phone: (718) 803-9602

#69
Lady Jay's
Cuisines: Bar
Average price: Inexpensive
Area: Williamsburg - North Side
Address: 633 Grand St
Brooklyn, NY 11211
Phone: (718) 387-1029

#70
O'Sullivan's Bar & Grill
Cuisines: Pub, American
Average price: Inexpensive
Area: Fort Hamilton, Bay Ridge
Address: 8902 3rd Ave
Brooklyn, NY 11209
Phone: (718) 745-9619

#71
Gramercy Park Bar
Cuisines: Pub, Wine Bar, Lounge
Average price: Modest
Area: Gramercy
Address: 322 2nd Ave
Manhattan, NY 10003
Phone: (646) 484-6948

#72
Mirrors On Grand
Cuisines: Bar
Average price: Inexpensive
Area: Clinton Hill
Address: 284 Grand Ave
Brooklyn, NY 11238
Phone: (718) 622-2277

#73
Skinny Dennis
Cuisines: Bar, Music Venues
Average price: Inexpensive
Area: Williamsburg - North Side
Address: 152 Metropolitan Ave
Brooklyn, NY 11249
Phone: (212) 555-1212

#74
Sunny's Bar
Cuisines: Bar
Average price: Inexpensive
Area: Red Hook
Address: 253 Conover St
Brooklyn, NY 11231
Phone: (718) 625-8211

#75
Lucey's Lounge
Cuisines: Lounge, Cocktail Bar
Average price: Modest
Area: Gowanus
Address: 475 3rd Ave
Brooklyn, NY 11231
Phone: (718) 877-1075

#76
The Peacock
Cuisines: British, Cocktail Bar
Average price: Expensive
Area: Midtown East, Murray Hill
Address: 24 E 39th St
New York, NY 10016
Phone: (646) 837-6776

#77
Shadow Lounge
Cuisines: Lounge, Mediterranean, Hookah Bar
Average price: Expensive
Area: Gravesend, Midwood
Address: 2085 Coney Island Ave
Brooklyn, NY 11223
Phone: (917) 933-4555

#78
Layaly Cafe
Cuisines: Mediterranean, Hookah Bar, Lounge
Average price: Modest
Area: Astoria
Address: 4409 Broadway
Astoria, NY 11103
Phone: (718) 606-8778

#79
Lea Wine Bar
Cuisines: Wine Bar, Lounge, Tapas
Average price: Modest
Area: Midtown East
Address: 230 Park Ave
New York, NY 10169
Phone: (212) 922-1546

#80
The Spot
Cuisines: Bar
Average price: Exclusive
Area: South Village
Address: 246 Spring St
New York, NY 10013
Phone: (212) 842-5500

#81
Madison Club Lounge
Cuisines: Lounge
Average price: Expensive
Area: Midtown East
Address: 45 East 45th St
New York, NY 10017
Phone: (212) 661-9600

#82
Above 6 At 6 Columbus
Cuisines: Lounge
Average price: Modest
Area: Hell's Kitchen, Midtown West
Address: 6 Columbus Cir
Manhattan, NY 10019
Phone: (212) 397-0404

#83
Bar Sardine
Cuisines: American, Bar
Average price: Modest
Area: West Village
Address: 183 W 10th St
New York, NY 10014
Phone: (646) 360-3705

#84
Minibar
Cuisines: Wine Bar, Lounge
Average price: Modest
Area: Carroll Gardens
Address: 482 Court St
Brooklyn, NY 11231
Phone: (718) 569-2321

#85
Jalopy Tavern
Cuisines: Bar, American
Average price: Modest
Area: Columbia Street Waterfront District
Address: 317 Columbia St
Brooklyn, NY 11231
Phone: (718) 395-3214

#86
Dick & Jane's Bar
Cuisines: Bar
Average price: Expensive
Area: Fort Greene
Address: 266 Adelphi St
Brooklyn, NY 11205
Phone: (347) 227-8021

#87
Clandestino
Cuisines: Bar
Average price: Modest
Area: Chinatown, Lower East Side
Address: 35 Canal St
New York, NY 10002
Phone: (212) 475-5505

#88
Tip Top Bar & Grill
Cuisines: Dive Bar
Average price: Inexpensive
Area: Bedford Stuyvesant, Clinton Hill
Address: 432 Franklin Ave
Brooklyn, NY 11238
Phone: (718) 857-9744

#89
Palace Cafe
Cuisines: Bar
Average price: Inexpensive
Area: Greenpoint
Address: 206 Nassau Ave
Brooklyn, NY 11222
Phone: (718) 383-9848

#90
Central Station
Cuisines: Bar, American
Average price: Modest
Area: Bushwick
Address: 84 Central Ave
Brooklyn, NY 11206
Phone: (718) 483-9884

#91
Blueprint
Cuisines: Cocktail Bar
Average price: Modest
Area: Park Slope
Address: 196 5th Ave
Brooklyn, NY 11217
Phone: (718) 622-6644

#92
Proper West
Cuisines: Sports Bar, American, Lounge
Average price: Modest
Area: Midtown West
Address: 54 W 39th St
New York, NY 10018
Phone: (212) 997-9000

#93
Bergen Hill
Cuisines: Cocktail Bar, Seafood
Average price: Expensive
Area: Carroll Gardens
Address: 387 Ct St
Brooklyn, NY 11231
Phone: (718) 858-5483

#94
Passenger Bar
Cuisines: Lounge
Average price: Modest
Area: Williamsburg - South Side
Address: 229 Roebling St
New York, NY 11211
Phone: (718) 218-7869

#95
Malbec and Tango House
Cuisines: Wine Bar, American
Average price: Exclusive
Area: NoHo
Address: 428 Lafayette St
New York, NY 10003
Phone: (212) 419-4645

#96
Underbar
Cuisines: Lounge
Average price: Expensive
Area: Union Square, Flatiron
Address: 201 Park Ave S
New York, NY 10003
Phone: (212) 358-1560

#97
St. Mazie
Cuisines: Bar, Comfort Food, Music Venues
Average price: Modest
Area: Williamsburg - North Side
Address: 345 Grand St Williamsburg
Brooklyn, NY 11211
Phone: (718) 384-4807

#98
The Mark Hotel Bar
Cuisines: Lounge
Average price: Expensive
Area: Upper East Side
Address: 25 E 77th
Manhattan, NY 10075
Phone: (212) 744-4300

#99
Anotheroom
Cuisines: Lounge
Average price: Modest
Area: TriBeCa
Address: 249 W Broadway
New York, NY 10013
Phone: (212) 226-1418

#100
Boilermaker
Cuisines: American, Cocktail Bar
Average price: Modest
Area: East Village
Address: 13 First Ave
New York, NY 10003
Phone: (212) 995-5400

#101
Akariba
Cuisines: Japanese, Bar
Average price: Modest
Area: Williamsburg - North Side
Address: 77 N 6th St
Brooklyn, NY 11211
Phone: (718) 388-6160

#102
Eastwood
Cuisines: Bar, American
Average price: Modest
Area: Lower East Side
Address: 221 E Broadway
New York, NY 10002
Phone: (212) 233-0124

#103
Maslow 6
Cuisines: Beer, Wine, Spirits, Wine Bar
Average price: Modest
Area: TriBeCa
Address: 211B W Broadway
New York, NY 10013
Phone: (212) 226-3127

#104
Central Restaurant Lounge & Bar
Cuisines: Sushi Bar, Lounge,
Event Planning, Service
Average price: Exclusive
Area: Steinway
Address: 2030 Steinway St
Astoria, NY 11105
Phone: (718) 726-1600

#105
Icon Bar
Cuisines: Gay Bar
Average price: Modest
Area: Astoria
Address: 31-84 33rd St
Astoria, NY 11106
Phone: (347) 808-7592

#106
American Cheez
Cuisines: Pizza, Dive Bar
Average price: Inexpensive
Area: South Slope, Park Slope
Address: 444 7th Ave
New York, NY 11215
Phone: (347) 725-4665

#107
The Electric Room
Cuisines: Bar
Average price: Exclusive
Area: Chelsea
Address: 335 W 16th St
New York, NY 10011
Phone: (212) 229-1269

#108
Henry's Rooftop Bar
Cuisines: American, Bar
Average price: Modest
Area: Midtown East
Address: 501 Lexington Ave
New York, NY 10017
Phone: (212) 755-1400

#109
Bar Nine
Cuisines: Lounge, Dive Bar, Piano Bar
Average price: Modest
Area: Hell's Kitchen, Midtown West, Theater District
Address: 807 9th Ave
New York, NY 10019
Phone: (212) 399-9336

#110
Sweetleaf
Cuisines: Coffee, Tea, Cocktail Bar
Average price: Modest
Area: Hunters Point
Address: 4615 Center Blvd
Long Island City, NY 11101
Phone: (347) 527-1038

#111
Supercollider
Cuisines: Lounge, Coffee, Tea
Average price: Inexpensive
Area: South Slope
Address: 609 4th Ave
Brooklyn, NY 11215
Phone: (347) 725-3419

#112
B61
Cuisines: Dive Bar
Average price: Modest
Area: Columbia Street Waterfront District
Address: 187 Columbia St
Brooklyn, NY 11231
Phone: (718) 643-5400

#113
Sky Terrace at Hudson
Cuisines: Lounge
Average price: Expensive
Area: Hell's Kitchen, Midtown West
Address: 356 W 58th Street
New York, NY 10019
Phone: (212) 554-6000

#114
54 Below
Cuisines: Jazz, Blues, Lounge
Average price: Expensive
Area: Midtown West, Theater District
Address: 254 W 54th St
New York, NY 10019
Phone: (866) 468-7619

#115
Salon de Lafayette
Cuisines: Bar, American
Average price: Expensive
Area: SoHo
Address: 157 Lafayette St
New York, NY 10013
Phone: (212) 925-1690

#116
PIPS
Cuisines: Sports Club, Art Gallery, Bar
Average price: Inexpensive
Area: Williamsburg - North Side
Address: 158 Roebling St
Brooklyn, NY 11211
Phone: (347) 674-7706

#117
The Winslow
Cuisines: Bar
Average price: Modest
Area: Gramercy
Address: 243 E 14th St
New York, NY 10003
Phone: (212) 777-7717

#118
Baby Grand
Cuisines: Karaoke, Lounge
Average price: Modest
Area: SoHo
Address: 161 Lafayette St
New York, NY 10013
Phone: (212) 219-8110

#119
Lounge 108
Cuisines: Lounge
Average price: Modest
Area: East Harlem
Address: 181 E 108th St
New York, NY 10029
Phone: (212) 876-6566

#120
Hombres Lounge
Cuisines: Gay Bar
Average price: Modest
Area: Jackson Heights
Address: 85-28 37th Ave
Jackson Heights, NY 11372
Phone: (718) 930-0886

#121
MASQ BAR
Cuisines: Lounge, American
Average price: Modest
Area: Midtown East
Address: 306 E 49th St
New York, NY 10017
Phone: (212) 644-8294

#122
The Royal Palms Shuffleboard Club
Cuisines: Social Club, Bar, Recreation Center
Average price: Modest
Area: Gowanus
Address: 514 Union St
Brooklyn, NY 11215
Phone: (347) 223-4410

#123
At the Wallace
Cuisines: Bar
Average price: Inexpensive
Area: Harlem
Address: 3612 Broadway
New York, NY 10031
Phone: (212) 234-6896

#124
South
Cuisines: Bar
Average price: Inexpensive
Area: South Slope
Address: 629 5th Ave
Brooklyn, NY 11215
Phone: (718) 832-4720

#125
Uncle Barry's
Cuisines: Pub
Average price: Inexpensive
Area: Park Slope
Address: 58 5th Ave
Brooklyn, NY 11217
Phone: (718) 622-4980

#126
Broken Land
Cuisines: Bar
Average price: Modest
Area: Greenpoint
Address: 105 Franklin St
Brooklyn, NY 11222
Phone: (718) 349-2901

#127
Formerly Crow's Bar
Cuisines: American, Pub
Average price: Modest
Area: Greenwich Village
Address: 85 Washington Pl
Manhattan, NY 10011
Phone: (212) 361-0077

#128
The Emerson
Cuisines: Lounge
Average price: Modest
Area: Bedford Stuyvesant, Clinton Hill
Address: 561 Myrtle Ave
Brooklyn, NY 11205
Phone: (347) 763-1310

#129
Amarachi Prime
Cuisines: Lounge, Breakfast & Brunch
Average price: Modest
Area: Downtown Brooklyn
Address: 189 Bridge St
Brooklyn, NY 11201
Phone: (718) 222-1010

#130
The Roost
Cuisines: Bar, Café
Average price: Modest
Area: East Village, Alphabet City
Address: 222 Ave B
New York, NY 10009
Phone: (646) 918-6700

#131
White Oak Tavern
Cuisines: Bar, American
Average price: Modest
Area: Greenwich Village
Address: 21 Waverly Pl
New York, NY 10003
Phone: (212) 260-2604

#132
Bar On
Cuisines: Lounge
Average price: Modest
Area: Chinatown, Civic Center
Address: 45 Mott St
New York, NY 10013
Phone: (212) 577-8880

#133
Montauk Club
Cuisines: American, Lounge
Average price: Expensive
Area: Park Slope, Prospect Heights
Address: 25 8th Ave
Brooklyn, NY 11201
Phone: (718) 638-0800

#134
RPM Bar
Cuisines: Bar
Average price: Inexpensive
Area: Lower East Side
Address: 266 Broome St
New York, NY 10013
Phone: (646) 918-6529

#135
Pata Paplean Bar
Cuisines: Bar
Average price: Modest
Area: Elmhurst
Address: 76-21 Woodside Ave
Elmhurst, NY 11373
Phone: (718) 651-2076

#136
Flute Midtown
Cuisines: Lounge, Champagne Bar
Average price: Expensive
Area: Midtown West, Theater District
Address: 205 W 54th St
New York, NY 10019
Phone: (212) 265-5169

#137
The Sky Deck
Cuisines: Bar, Burgers
Average price: Expensive
Area: Midtown West, Theater District
Address: 226 West 52nd Street
Manhattan, NY 10019
Phone: (212) 315-0100

#138
Shayz Lounge
Cuisines: Pub
Average price: Modest
Area: Greenpoint
Address: 130 Franklin St
Brooklyn, NY 11222
Phone: (718) 389-3888

#139
Jasmin Lounge
Cuisines: Egyptian, Lounge
Average price: Inexpensive
Area: Astoria
Address: 2550 Steinway St
New York, NY 11103
Phone: (646) 251-0493

#140
BAM Café
Cuisines: Lounge, Music Venues
Average price: Modest
Area: Fort Greene
Address: 30 Lafayette Ave
Brooklyn, NY 11217
Phone: (718) 623-7811

#141
The Late Late
Cuisines: Pub
Average price: Modest
Area: Lower East Side
Address: 159 E Houston St
New York, NY 10005
Phone: (646) 861-3342

#142
The Crow's Nest
Cuisines: Bar
Average price: Modest
Area: Kips Bay, Stuyvesant Town
Address: The E River at 30th St
New York, NY 10016
Phone: (212) 683-3333

#143
Bar Pleiades
Cuisines: Bar
Average price: Exclusive
Area: Yorkville, Upper East Side
Address: 20 E 76th St
New York, NY 10021
Phone: (212) 772-2600

#144
Brooklyn Stoops
Cuisines: Breakfast & Brunch, Bar
Average price: Inexpensive
Area: Bedford Stuyvesant
Address: 748 Myrtle Ave
Brooklyn, NY 11205
Phone: (347) 378-2505

#145
Flute Gramercy
Cuisines: Lounge, Champagne Bar, Music Venues
Average price: Expensive
Area: Flatiron
Address: 40 E 20th St
New York, NY 10003
Phone: (212) 529-7870

#146
Caledonia Scottish Pub
Cuisines: Pub, Scottish
Average price: Modest
Area: Yorkville, Upper East Side
Address: 1609 2nd Ave
New York, NY 10028
Phone: (212) 879-0402

#147
Frank's Cocktail Lounge
Cuisines: Lounge
Average price: Modest
Area: Fort Greene
Address: 660 Fulton St
Brooklyn, NY 11217
Phone: (718) 625-9339

#148
Mary's Bar
Cuisines: Pub
Average price: Modest
Area: South Slope
Address: 708 5th Ave
Brooklyn, NY 11215
Phone: (718) 499-2175

#149
Bar Sepia
Cuisines: Bar
Average price: Modest
Area: Prospect Heights
Address: 234 Underhill Ave
Brooklyn, NY 11238
Phone: (718) 399-6680

#150
Holland Bar
Cuisines: Dive Bar, Sports Bar
Average price: Inexpensive
Area: Hell's Kitchen, Midtown West
Address: 532 Ninth Ave
New York, NY 10018
Phone: (212) 502-4609

#151
Roof at Park South
Cuisines: Cocktail Bar
Average price: Expensive
Area: Flatiron
Address: 125 E 27th St
New York, NY 10016
Phone: (212) 204-5222

#152
The Grand National
Cuisines: Sports Bar
Average price: Modest
Area: East Williamsburg
Address: 524 Grand St
Brooklyn, NY 11211
Phone: (347) 725-4386

#153
Desert Rain Lounge
Cuisines: Lounge, Hookah Bar
Average price: Modest
Area: Forest Hills
Address: 107-29 Metropolitan Ave
Forest Hills, NY 11375
Phone: (718) 880-1854

#154
Wise Men
Cuisines: American, Cocktail Bar
Average price: Modest
Area: East Village, NoHo
Address: 355 Bowery
New York, NY 10003
Phone: (646) 590-4244

#155
Rocky McBride's
Cuisines: Sports Bar, Pub
Average price: Modest
Area: Astoria
Address: 27-01 23rd Ave
Astoria, NY 11105
Phone: (718) 777-2723

#156
Refinery Rooftop
Cuisines: Lounge
Average price: Expensive
Area: Midtown West
Address: 63 W 38th St
New York, NY 10018
Phone: (646) 664-0310

#157
The Owl's Head
Cuisines: Wine Bar
Average price: Modest
Area: Bay Ridge
Address: 479 74th St
Brooklyn, NY 11209
Phone: (718) 680-2436

#158
Archer Hotel New York
Cuisines: Hotel, Bar, Restaurant
Average price: Expensive
Area: Midtown West
Address: 45 West 38th Street
New York, NY 10018
Phone: (212) 719-4100

#159
Forrest Point
Cuisines: Bar, American, Sandwiches
Average price: Modest
Area: East Williamsburg, Bushwick
Address: 970 Flushing Ave
Brooklyn, NY 11206
Phone: (718) 366-2742

#160
The NoMad Library
Cuisines: Gastropub, Lounge
Average price: Expensive
Area: Flatiron
Address: 1170 Broadway & 28th St
New York, NY 10001
Phone: (347) 472-5660

#161
Amaru Pisco Bar
Cuisines: Bar
Average price: Modest
Area: Jackson Heights
Address: 84-13 Northern Blvd
Jackson Heights, NY 11372
Phone: (718) 205-5577

#162
Pioneers
Cuisines: Lounge, Pub, Venues, Event Space
Average price: Modest
Area: Chelsea, Midtown West
Address: 138 W 29th St
New York, NY 10001
Phone: (212) 714-2222

#163
Banter
Cuisines: Bar
Average price: Modest
Area: Williamsburg - South Side
Address: 132 Havemeyer St
Brooklyn, NY 11211
Phone: (718) 599-5200

#164
Spanky & Darla's
Cuisines: Bar
Average price: Inexpensive
Area: East Village
Address: 140 1st Ave
Manhattan, NY 10009
Phone: (212) 254-6631

#165
Bearded Lady
Cuisines: Bar
Average price: Modest
Area: Prospect Heights
Address: 686A Washington Ave
Brooklyn, NY 11238
Phone: (469) 232-7333

#166
Aziza Cafe & Lounge
Cuisines: Hookah Bar, Lounge, Café
Average price: Modest
Area: East Village
Address: 45 1st Ave
New York, NY 10003
Phone: (212) 777-3778

#167
Anable Basin Sailing Bar & Grill
Cuisines: Bar, Brazilian
Average price: Modest
Area: Hunters Point
Address: 4-40 44th Dr
Long Island City, NY 11101
Phone: (646) 207-1333

#168
Littlefield
Cuisines: Performing Arts, Art Gallery, Bar
Average price: Modest
Area: Gowanus
Address: 622 Degraw St
Brooklyn, NY 11217
Phone: (718) 855-3388

#169
67 Orange Street
Cuisines: Lounge, Cocktail Bar
Average price: Expensive
Area: Harlem
Address: 2082 Frederick Douglas Blvd
New York, NY 10026
Phone: (212) 662-2030

#170
The Skylark
Cuisines: Cocktail Bar
Average price: Expensive
Area: Midtown West
Address: 200 W 39th St
New York, NY 10018
Phone: (212) 257-4578

#171
Paddy Reilly's Music Bar
Cuisines: Pub, Music Venues, Irish Pub
Average price: Modest
Area: Midtown East, Kips Bay
Address: 519 2nd Ave
New York, NY 10016
Phone: (212) 686-1210

#172
Corkbuzz Chelsea Market
Cuisines: Wine Bar
Average price: Expensive
Area: Chelsea, Meatpacking District
Address: 75 9th Ave
New York, NY 10011
Phone: (646) 237-4847

#173
The Saint Catherine
Cuisines: American, Bar
Average price: Modest
Area: Prospect Heights
Address: 660 Washington Ave
Brooklyn, NY 11238
Phone: (347) 663-9316

#174
Townhouse 275
Cuisines: Cocktail Bar
Average price: Modest
Area: Fort Hamilton, Bay Ridge
Address: 275 94th St
Brooklyn, NY 11209
Phone: (347) 560-4001

#175
Drunken Munkey NYC
Cuisines: Indian, Cocktail Bar
Average price: Modest
Area: Yorkville, Upper East Side
Address: 338 E 92nd St
New York, NY 10128
Phone: (646) 998-4600

#176
The Library at The Public
Cuisines: American, Lounge, Sandwiches
Average price: Expensive
Area: East Village, NoHo
Address: 425 Lafayette St
New York, NY 10003
Phone: (212) 539-8777

#177
Against the Grain
Cuisines: Bar
Average price: Modest
Area: East Village, Alphabet City
Address: 620 E 6th St
New York, NY 10009
Phone: (212) 358-7065

#178
Sweetwater Social
Cuisines: Cocktail Bar, Sports Bar, Lounge
Average price: Modest
Area: Greenwich Village
Address: 643 Broadway
New York, NY 10012
Phone: (212) 253-0477

#179
M White Bar
Cuisines: Bar
Average price: Modest
Area: East Village, Alphabet City
Address: 448 E 13th St
New York, NY 10009
Phone: (646) 746-1357

#180
Baby's All Right
Cuisines: Bar, Music Venues, American
Average price: Modest
Area: South Williamsburg
Address: 146 Broadway
Brooklyn, NY 11211
Phone: (718) 599-5800

#181
Montero's Bar & Grill
Cuisines: Dive Bar, American
Average price: Inexpensive
Area: Brooklyn Heights, Cobble Hill
Address: 73 Atlantic Ave
Brooklyn, NY 11201
Phone: (646) 729-4129

#182
Nebu Hookah Lounge
Cuisines: Hookah Bar, Lounge, Champagne Bar
Average price: Inexpensive
Area: Woodhaven
Address: 86-72 80th St
Woodhaven, NY 11421
Phone: (347) 881-7700

#183
Rocky Sullivan's
Cuisines: Irish, Pub
Average price: Inexpensive
Area: Red Hook
Address: 34 Van Dyke St
Brooklyn, NY 11231
Phone: (718) 246-8050

#184
The Gilroy
Cuisines: Cocktail Bar, American
Average price: Expensive
Area: Yorkville, Upper East Side
Address: 1561 2nd Ave
New York, NY 10028
Phone: (212) 734-8800

#185
Ba'sik
Cuisines: Cocktail Bar, Salad, Sandwiches
Average price: Modest
Area: Williamsburg - North Side
Address: 323 Graham Ave
Brooklyn, NY 11211
Phone: (347) 889-7597

#186
Havana Social
Cuisines: Caribbean, Cuban, Cocktail Bar
Average price: Modest
Area: Hell's Kitchen, Midtown West
Address: 688 10th Ave
New York, NY 10019
Phone: (212) 956-2155

#187
Atera
Cuisines: American, Lounge
Average price: Exclusive
Area: Civic Center, TriBeCa
Address: 77 Worth St
New York, NY 10013
Phone: (212) 226-1444

#188
Upright Brew House
Cuisines: American, Bar
Average price: Modest
Area: West Village
Address: 547 Hudson St
New York, NY 10014
Phone: (212) 810-9944

#189
The Diamond
Cuisines: Bar, Beer, Wine, Spirits
Average price: Modest
Area: Greenpoint
Address: 43 Franklin St
Brooklyn, NY 11222
Phone: (718) 383-5030

#190
Sweet Science
Cuisines: Bar, Burgers, American
Average price: Modest
Area: East Williamsburg
Address: 135 Graham Ave
Brooklyn, NY 11206
Phone: (347) 763-0872

#191
Harlem on Fifth
Cuisines: American, Comedy Club, Hookah Bar
Average price: Modest
Area: East Harlem
Address: 2150 5th Ave
New York, NY 10037
Phone: (212) 234-5600

#192
Botanica
Cuisines: Bar
Average price: Modest
Area: Red Hook
Address: 220 Conover St
Brooklyn, NY 11231
Phone: (347) 225-0148

#193
Biblio
Cuisines: Bar, American, Gastropub
Average price: Modest
Area: Williamsburg - North Side
Address: 149 N 6th St
Brooklyn, NY 11211
Phone: (718) 384-8200

#194
Matt Torrey's
Cuisines: Bar
Average price: Modest
Area: East Williamsburg
Address: 46 Bushwick Ave
Brooklyn, NY 11211
Phone: (718) 218-7646

#195
Proletariat
Cuisines: Bar
Average price: Modest
Area: East Village, Alphabet City
Address: 102 St Marks Pl
New York, NY 10009
Phone: (212) 777-6707

#196
Tavern Lounge
Cuisines: Night Club, Sports Bar, Lounge
Average price: Inexpensive
Area: Richmond Hill
Address: 9707 Jamaica Ave
Woodhaven, NY 11421
Phone: (718) 673-5659

#197
5 Bar Karaoke & Lounge
Cuisines: Karaoke, Lounge, Sports Bar
Average price: Modest
Area: Midtown West, Koreatown
Address: 38 W 32 St
New York, NY 10016
Phone: (212) 594-6644

#198
A60
Cuisines: Lounge
Average price: Expensive
Area: South Village
Address: 60 Thompson St
New York, NY 10012
Phone: (877) 431-0400

#199
Ramona
Cuisines: Cocktail Bar
Average price: Modest
Area: Greenpoint
Address: 113 Franklin St
Brooklyn, NY 11222
Phone: (347) 227-8164

#200
Project Parlor
Cuisines: Lounge
Average price: Modest
Area: Bedford Stuyvesant
Address: 742 Myrtle Ave
Brooklyn, NY 11205
Phone: (347) 497-0550

#201
Fayrooz Hookah Lounge & Bar
Cuisines: Halal, Hookah Bar, Lounge
Average price: Modest
Area: Astoria
Address: 2808 Steinway St
Astoria, NY 11103
Phone: (718) 204-7667

#202
The Tank
Cuisines: Music Venues, Performing Arts
Average price: Inexpensive
Area: Midtown West, Theater District
Address: 151 W 46th St
New York, NY 10036
Phone: (212) 563-6269

#203
Juga Lounge
Cuisines: Lounge
Average price: Modest
Area: Midtown West
Address: 8 W 36th St
New York, NY 10018
Phone: (212) 290-2211

#204
Nublu
Cuisines: Bar, Music Venues
Average price: Modest
Area: East Village, Alphabet City
Address: 62 Ave C
New York, NY 10009
Phone: (646) 546-5206

#205
Middle Branch
Cuisines: Bar
Average price: Modest
Area: Midtown East, Murray Hill, Kips Bay
Address: 154 E 33rd St
New York, NY 10016
Phone: (212) 213-1350

#206
Sunita Bar
Cuisines: Lounge
Average price: Modest
Area: Lower East Side
Address: 106 Norfolk St
New York, NY 10002
Phone: (212) 253-8860

#207
Coal Yard Bar
Cuisines: Bar
Average price: Inexpensive
Area: East Village
Address: 102 1st Ave
New York, NY 10009
Phone: (212) 677-4595

#208
Hayaty
Cuisines: Hookah Bar, Middle Eastern
Average price: Modest
Area: East Village, Alphabet City
Address: 103 Ave A
New York, NY 10009
Phone: (212) 388-0588

#209
Gotham City Lounge
Cuisines: Dive Bar
Average price: Inexpensive
Area: Bushwick
Address: 1293 Myrtle Ave
Brooklyn, NY 11221
Phone: (718) 387-4182

#210
Red Velvet Lounge
Cuisines: Lounge
Average price: Modest
Area: Lower East Side
Address: 174 Rivington St
New York, NY 10002
Phone: (212) 260-2220

#211
The Drunken Horse
Cuisines: Wine Bar, Turkish
Average price: Modest
Area: Chelsea
Address: 225 10th Ave
New York, NY 10011
Phone: (212) 604-0505

#212
The Loopy Doopy Rooftop Bar
Cuisines: Lounge
Average price: Expensive
Area: Battery Park
Address: 102 N End Ave
New York, NY 10282
Phone: (646) 769-4627

#213
The Shakespeare
Cuisines: Pub, British
Average price: Modest
Area: Midtown East, Murray Hill
Address: 24 E 39th St
New York, NY 10016
Phone: (646) 837-6779

#214
The Otheroom
Cuisines: Lounge, Wine Bar, American
Average price: Modest
Area: West Village
Address: 143 Perry St
New York, NY 10014
Phone: (212) 645-9758

#215
Measure
Cuisines: Lounge, Jazz, Blues, Tapas
Average price: Expensive
Area: Midtown West
Address: 400 5th Ave
New York, NY 10018
Phone: (212) 695-4005

#216
East Village Social
Cuisines: Bar, American
Average price: Modest
Area: East Village, Alphabet City
Address: 126 St Marks St
New York, NY 10009
Phone: (646) 755-8662

#217
St Ann's Warehouse
Cuisines: Performing Arts, Music Venues
Average price: Modest
Area: DUMBO
Address: 29 Jay St.
Brooklyn, NY 11201
Phone: (718) 254-8779

#218
Serena's Wine Bar Cafe
Cuisines: Wine Bar, Café
Average price: Modest
Area: Upper East Side
Address: 1268 2nd Ave
New York, NY 10065
Phone: (212) 988-2646

#219
Vu 46
Cuisines: Lounge
Average price: Inexpensive
Area: Midtown West
Address: 59 W 46th St, 14th Fl
New York, NY 10036
Phone: (212) 382-3045

#220
Judy & Punch
Cuisines: Cocktail Bar
Average price: Modest
Area: Astoria
Address: 34-08 30th Ave
Queens, NY 11103
Phone: (718) 626-3100

#221
The Milling Room
Cuisines: American, Bar, Desserts
Average price: Expensive
Area: Upper West Side
Address: 446 Columbus Ave
New York, NY 10024
Phone: (212) 595-0380

#222
The Great Georgiana
Cuisines: Bar
Average price: Modest
Area: Fort Greene, Clinton Hill
Address: 248 Dekalb Ave
Brooklyn, NY 11205
Phone: (718) 362-7569

#223
Lowlands Bar
Cuisines: Bar
Average price: Inexpensive
Area: Gowanus
Address: 543 3rd Ave
Brooklyn, NY 11215
Phone: (347) 463-9458

#224
il Vino Wine Bar
Cuisines: Wine Bar, Italian, American
Average price: Modest
Area: Yorkville, Upper East Side
Address: 1728 2nd Ave
New York, NY 10128
Phone: (212) 426-0919

#225
Brooklyn Tavern
Cuisines: Bar
Average price: Inexpensive
Area: Boerum Hill
Address: 31 3rd Ave
Brooklyn, NY 11217
Phone: (718) 797-0677

#226
The Quays Pub
Cuisines: Pub
Average price: Inexpensive
Area: Astoria
Address: 45-02 30th Ave
Astoria, NY 11103
Phone: (718) 204-8435

#227
Three Jolly Pigeons
Cuisines: Pub
Average price: Inexpensive
Area: Bay Ridge
Address: 6802 3rd Ave
Brooklyn, NY 11226
Phone: (718) 745-9350

#228
Astoria Tavern
Cuisines: Pub
Average price: Inexpensive
Area: Astoria
Address: 33-16 23rd Ave
Astoria, NY 11105
Phone: (347) 813-4954

#229
The Archive
Cuisines: Bar
Average price: Modest
Area: Midtown East
Address: 12 E 36th St
New York, NY 10016
Phone: (212) 213-0093

#230
Vinus and Marc
Cuisines: Breakfast & Brunch, Cocktail Bar
Average price: Modest
Area: Yorkville, Upper East Side
Address: 1825 Second Ave
New York, NY 10128
Phone: (646) 692-9105

#231
Gallagher's 2000
Cuisines: Adult Entertainment, Lounge
Average price: Modest
Area: Sunnyside
Address: 43-19 37th St
Long Island City, NY 11101
Phone: (718) 361-1348

#232
Maspeth Ale House
Cuisines: Bar
Average price: Modest
Area: Maspeth
Address: 64 -14 Grand Ave
Maspeth, NY 11378
Phone: (718) 894-8100

#233
Flute East
Cuisines: Champagne Bar
Average price: Modest
Area: Midtown East
Address: 303 E 53 St
New York, NY 10022
Phone: (646) 998-5434

#234
Hunkamania NYC
Cuisines: Adult Entertainment
Average price: Modest
Area: Midtown West
Address: 200 W 39th St
New York, NY 10018
Phone: (917) 921-8476

#235
Bantry Bay Publik House
Cuisines: Pub, Gastropub, Irish
Average price: Modest
Area: Sunnyside
Address: 3301 Greenpoint Ave
Long Island City, NY 11101
Phone: (718) 784-9500

#236
The Barn
Cuisines: Bar
Average price: Modest
Area: Astoria
Address: 30-09 21st St
Astoria, NY 11102
Phone: (718) 728-0305

#237
Brandy's Piano Bar
Cuisines: Bar, Music Venues
Average price: Modest
Area: Yorkville, Upper East Side
Address: 235 E 84th St
New York, NY 10028
Phone: (212) 744-4949

#238
Tradesman
Cuisines: Bar
Average price: Modest
Area: East Williamsburg
Address: 222 Bushwick Ave
Brooklyn, NY 11206
Phone: (718) 386-5300

#239
Deja Vu
Cuisines: Lounge, Wine Bar, Hookah Bar
Average price: Modest
Area: Astoria
Address: 33-22 28th Ave
Astoria, NY 11103
Phone: (718) 267-8212

#240
The Fulton Grand
Cuisines: Bar
Average price: Modest
Area: Clinton Hill
Address: 1011 Fulton St
Brooklyn, NY 11238
Phone: (718) 399-2240

#241
The Fifth Estate
Cuisines: Bar, Music Venues
Average price: Inexpensive
Area: South Slope, Park Slope
Address: 506 5th Ave
Brooklyn, NY 11215
Phone: (718) 840-0089

#242
Lucy's Whey
Cuisines: Cheese Shop, Café, Wine Bar
Average price: Expensive
Area: Upper East Side
Address: 1417 Lexington Ave
New York, NY 10128
Phone: (212) 289-8900

#243
Murray Bar
Cuisines: American, Sports Bar
Average price: Modest
Area: Midtown East, Murray Hill
Address: 58 E 34th St
New York, NY 10016
Phone: (646) 590-8463

#244
The Gaslight
Cuisines: Pub
Average price: Inexpensive
Area: Sunnyside
Address: 4317 Queens Blvd
Sunnyside, NY 11104
Phone: (718) 729-9900

#245
B Side
Cuisines: Dive Bar
Average price: Inexpensive
Area: East Village, Alphabet City
Address: 204 Ave B
New York, NY 10009
Phone: (212) 475-4600

#246
Barzinho
Cuisines: Brazilian, Bar
Average price: Modest
Area: Chinatown, Lower East Side
Address: 48 Hester St
New York, NY 10002
Phone: (917) 635-6911

#247
The Anchored Inn
Cuisines: Bar, American
Average price: Modest
Area: East Williamsburg
Address: 57 Waterbury St
Brooklyn, NY 11206
Phone: (718) 576-3297

#248
Bunga's Den
Cuisines: Dive Bar
Average price: Inexpensive
Area: Chelsea
Address: 137 W 14th St
New York, NY 10011
Phone: (212) 242-1040

#249
MUI
Cuisines: Japanese, Korean, Lounge
Average price: Modest
Area: Midtown West, Koreatown
Address: 10 W 32nd St
New York, NY 10001
Phone: (212) 244-1900

#250
The Bar Downstairs
Cuisines: Lounge, Tapas, Cocktail Bar
Average price: Expensive
Area: Midtown East
Address: 485 5th Ave
New York, NY 10017
Phone: (212) 601-1234

#251
Revision Lounge & Gallery
Cuisines: Lounge
Average price: Modest
Area: East Village, Alphabet City
Address: 219 Ave B
New York, NY 10009
Phone: (646) 490-7271

#252
Village Pisco
Cuisines: Cocktail Bar, Peruvian, American
Average price: Modest
Area: Greenwich Village
Address: 45 W 8th St
New York, NY 10011
Phone: (212) 995-2700

#253
The Third Man
Cuisines: Cocktail Bar
Average price: Modest
Area: East Village, Alphabet City
Address: 116 Ave C
New York, NY 10009
Phone: (212) 598-1040

#254
The Graham
Cuisines: Bar, Music Venues, Breakfast & Brunch
Average price: Inexpensive
Area: East Williamsburg
Address: 151 Meserole St
New York, NY 11206
Phone: (718) 388-4682

#255
Phil's Crummy Corner
Cuisines: Sports Bar, Latin American
Average price: Modest
Area: Columbia Street Waterfront District
Address: 323 Columbia St
Brooklyn, NY 11231
Phone: (718) 246-1252

#256
Doppio Artisan Bistro
Cuisines: Wine Bar, Italian, Pizza
Average price: Expensive
Area: West Village
Address: 581 Hudson St
New York, NY 10014
Phone: (212) 206-1444

#257
Delroys Cafe and Wine Bar
Cuisines: Café, Wine Bar
Average price: Modest
Area: Prospect Lefferts Gardens
Address: 65A Fenimore St
Brooklyn, NY 11225
Phone: (347) 715-6001

#258
Pinks
Cuisines: Cocktail Bar, American, Lounge
Average price: Modest
Area: East Village
Address: 242 E 10th St
Manhattan, NY 10003
Phone: (646) 918-6231

#259
Donna
Cuisines: Lounge, Cocktail Bar
Average price: Modest
Area: South Williamsburg
Address: 27 Broadway
Brooklyn, NY 11249
Phone: (646) 568-6622

#260
Veronica's Bar
Cuisines: Pub
Average price: Inexpensive
Area: Astoria, Long Island City
Address: 34-04 36th Ave
Astoria, NY 11106
Phone: (718) 729-9744

#261
Gramercy Park
Cuisines: Lounge
Average price: Modest
Area: Kips Bay, Flatiron
Address: 2 Lexington Ave
New York, NY 10010
Phone: (212) 920-3300

#262
Ghost
Cuisines: Lounge
Average price: Modest
Area: Lower East Side
Address: 132A Eldridge St
New York, NY 10002
Phone: (212) 775-8390

#263
Boobie Trap
Cuisines: Dive Bar
Average price: Inexpensive
Area: Bushwick
Address: 308 Bleecker St
Brooklyn, NY 11237
Phone: (347) 240-9105

#264
Deacon Brodie's
Cuisines: Pub
Average price: Modest
Area: Hell's Kitchen, Midtown West, Theater District
Address: 370 W 46th St
New York, NY 10036
Phone: (212) 262-1452

#265
Nurnberger Bierhalle
Cuisines: Bar, German
Average price: Inexpensive
Area: West Brighton
Address: 817 Castleton Ave
Staten Island, NY 10310
Phone: (718) 816-7461

#266
Iona
Cuisines: Bar
Average price: Modest
Area: Williamsburg - South Side, Williamsburg - North Side
Address: 180 Grand St
Brooklyn, NY 11211
Phone: (718) 384-5008

#267
Bar B
Cuisines: Italian, Bar
Average price: Modest
Area: Chelsea
Address: 84 7th Ave
New York, NY 10011
Phone: (212) 229-1888

#268
Heavy Woods
Cuisines: Bar, Café, Cajun, Creole
Average price: Modest
Area: Bushwick
Address: 50 Wyckoff Ave
New York, NY 11237
Phone: (929) 234-3500

#269
Lock Yard
Cuisines: American, Hot Dogs, Pub
Average price: Modest
Area: Fort Hamilton, Bay Ridge
Address: 9221 5th Ave
Brooklyn, NY 11209
Phone: (718) 333-5282

#270
2nd Floor on Clinton
Cuisines: Lounge
Average price: Expensive
Area: Lower East Side
Address: 67 Clinton St
New York, NY 10002
Phone: (212) 529-6900

#271
Dream Baby Bar & Cocktail Parlour
Cuisines: Cocktail Bar, Lounge
Average price: Modest
Area: East Village, Alphabet City
Address: 162-164 Ave B
New York, NY 10009
Phone: (646) 807-3754

#272
The Owl Farm
Cuisines: Pub
Average price: Modest
Area: Park Slope, Gowanus
Address: 297 9th St
Brooklyn, NY 11215
Phone: (718) 499-4988

#273
Wolf and Deer
Cuisines: Wine Bar, American
Average price: Modest
Area: Park Slope
Address: 74 5th Ave
Brooklyn, NY 11217
Phone: (718) 398-3181

#274
Miles
Cuisines: Wine Bar, American, Cocktail Bar
Average price: Modest
Area: Bushwick
Address: 101 Wilson Ave
Brooklyn, NY 11237
Phone: (718) 483-9172

#275
Fashion Rock
Cuisines: Venues, Event Space, Lounge
Average price: Modest
Area: Bedford Stuyvesant
Address: 491 Tompkins Ave
Brooklyn, NY 11216
Phone: (718) 808-2334

#276
Turnmill
Cuisines: Sports Bar, Pub, Lounge
Average price: Modest
Area: Flatiron
Address: 119 E 27th St
New York, NY 10016
Phone: (646) 524-6060

#277
Shigure
Cuisines: Japanese, Bar
Average price: Expensive
Area: TriBeCa
Address: 277 Church St
New York, NY 10013
Phone: (212) 965-0200

#278
Barbes
Cuisines: Bar, Jazz, Blues
Average price: Modest
Area: South Slope, Park Slope
Address: 376 9th St
Brooklyn, NY 11215
Phone: (347) 422-0248

#279
The Sackett
Cuisines: Bar
Average price: Modest
Area: Park Slope, Gowanus
Address: 661 Sackett St
Brooklyn, NY 11217
Phone: (718) 622-0437

#280
Tooker Alley
Cuisines: Lounge, Cocktail Bar
Average price: Modest
Area: Crown Heights, Prospect Heights
Address: 793 Washington Ave
Brooklyn, NY 11238
Phone: (347) 955-4743

#281
Maiden Lane
Cuisines: Seafood, Bar
Average price: Modest
Area: East Village, Alphabet City
Address: 162 Ave B
New York, NY 10009
Phone: (646) 755-8911

#282
One Star
Cuisines: Bar
Average price: Inexpensive
Area: Chelsea
Address: 147 W 24th St
New York, NY 10011
Phone: (212) 777-0100

#283
Alphabet City Beer Company
Cuisines: Bar, Beer, Wine, Spirits
Average price: Modest
Area: East Village, Alphabet City
Address: 96 Ave C
New York, NY 10009
Phone: (646) 422-7103

#284
Cafe Dancer
Cuisines: American, Café, Bar
Average price: Inexpensive
Area: Lower East Side
Address: 96 Orchard St
New York, NY 10002
Phone: (212) 677-1808

#285
Grand Bar & Lounge at Soho Grand Hotel
Cuisines: Lounge
Average price: Expensive
Area: South Village, SoHo, TriBeCa
Address: 310 W Broadway
New York, NY 10013
Phone: (212) 965-3588

#286
The Long Island Bar
Cuisines: Cocktail Bar, Lounge
Average price: Modest
Area: Cobble Hill
Address: 110 Atlantic Ave
New York, NY 11201
Phone: (718) 625-8908

#287
Irish Haven
Cuisines: Pub
Average price: Inexpensive
Area: Sunset Park
Address: 5721 4th Ave
Brooklyn, NY 11220
Phone: (718) 439-9893

#288
Ciccio
Cuisines: Italian, Bar
Average price: Modest
Area: South Village
Address: 190 6th Ave
New York, NY 10012
Phone: (646) 476-9498

#289
Bed-Vyne Brew
Cuisines: Wine Bar, Music Venues, Dive Bar
Average price: Modest
Area: Bedford Stuyvesant
Address: 370 Tompkins Ave
Brooklyn, NY 11216
Phone: (347) 915-1080

#290
Bizarre
Cuisines: Music Venues, Cocktail Bar
Average price: Modest
Area: Bushwick
Address: 12 Jefferson St
Brooklyn, NY 11206
Phone: (347) 915-2717

#291
Lantern's Keep
Cuisines: Cocktail Bar
Average price: Expensive
Area: Midtown West
Address: 49 W 44th St
New York, NY 10036
Phone: (212) 453-4287

#292
Temple Bar
Cuisines: Lounge, Tapas
Average price: Expensive
Area: NoHo
Address: 332 Lafayette St
New York, NY 10012
Phone: (212) 925-4242

#293
Friars Club
Cuisines: Nightlife, Restaurant
Average price: Exclusive
Area: Midtown East
Address: 57 E 55th St
New York, NY 10022
Phone: (212) 751-7272

#294
The Brooklyn Inn
Cuisines: Bar
Average price: Inexpensive
Area: Boerum Hill
Address: 138 Bergen St
Brooklyn, NY 11217
Phone: (718) 522-2525

#295
The Montrose
Cuisines: Pub, Sports Bar
Average price: Modest
Area: Park Slope
Address: 47 5th Ave
Brooklyn, NY 11217
Phone: (347) 763-0010

#296
William Barnacle Tavern
Cuisines: Bar
Average price: Modest
Area: East Village
Address: 80 St Mark's Pl
New York, NY 10009
Phone: (212) 388-0388

#297
Skylark Bar
Cuisines: Bar
Average price: Inexpensive
Area: South Slope, Park Slope
Address: 477 5th Ave
Brooklyn, NY 11215
Phone: (347) 227-8196

#298
The Freak Bar
Cuisines: Bar
Average price: Inexpensive
Area: Coney Island
Address: 1208 Surf Ave
New York, NY 11224
Phone: (718) 372-5159

#299
The Grand Victory
Cuisines: Music Venues, Bar
Average price: Inexpensive
Area: Williamsburg - South Side,
Williamsburg - North Side
Address: 245 Grand St
Brooklyn, NY 11211
Phone: (347) 529-6610

#300
The Three Diamond Door
Cuisines: Bar
Average price: Inexpensive
Area: Bushwick
Address: 211 Knickerbocker Ave
Brooklyn, NY 11237
Phone: (718) 576-6136

#301
Fish Bar
Cuisines: Restaurant, Bar
Average price: Inexpensive
Area: East Village
Address: 237 E 5th St
New York, NY 10003
Phone: (212) 475-4949

#302
Red 58
Cuisines: American, Lounge
Average price: Modest
Area: Midtown West
Address: 158 W 58th St
New York, NY 10019
Phone: (212) 245-0125

#303
The Second Chance Saloon
Cuisines: Pub
Average price: Inexpensive
Area: Williamsburg - North Side
Address: 659 Grand St
Brooklyn, NY 11211
Phone: (718) 387-4411

#304
Lone Wolf
Cuisines: Bar, Music Venues
Average price: Inexpensive
Area: Bedford Stuyvesant, Bushwick
Address: 1089 Broadway
Brooklyn, NY 11221
Phone: (718) 455-2028

#305
Trophy Bar
Cuisines: Night Club, Cocktail Bar, American
Average price: Inexpensive
Area: Williamsburg - South Side, South Williamsburg
Address: 351 Broadway
Brooklyn, NY 11211
Phone: (347) 227-8515

#306
Greenwich Street Tavern
Cuisines: American, Pub
Average price: Modest
Area: TriBeCa
Address: 399 Greenwich St
New York, NY 10013
Phone: (212) 334-7827

#307
Double Wide
Cuisines: Southern, Bar, Breakfast & Brunch
Average price: Modest
Area: East Village, Alphabet City
Address: 505 E 12th St
New York, NY 10009
Phone: (917) 261-6461

#308
The Black Hound
Cuisines: Lounge
Average price: Modest
Area: Battery Park
Address: 301 S End Ave
New York, NY 10280
Phone: (212) 945-0562

#309
Maracuja Bar & Grill
Cuisines: Lounge
Average price: Inexpensive
Area: Williamsburg - North Side
Address: 279 Grand St
Brooklyn, NY 11211
Phone: (718) 302-9023

#310
Farrell's
Cuisines: Bar
Average price: Inexpensive
Area: Windsor Terrace
Address: 215 Prospect Park W
Brooklyn, NY 11215
Phone: (718) 788-8779

#311
Bar Seven Five
Cuisines: Bar
Average price: Modest
Area: Financial District
Address: 75 Wall St
New York, NY 10005
Phone: (212) 590-1234

#312
The Porterhouse Brewing Company
Cuisines: Brewerie, Pub
Average price: Modest
Area: Financial District
Address: 58 Pearl St
New York, NY 10004
Phone: (212) 968-1776

#313
Greenpoint Heights
Cuisines: Bar, American
Average price: Modest
Area: Greenpoint
Address: 278 Nassau Ave
Brooklyn, NY 11222
Phone: (718) 389-0110

#314
Club Macanudo
Cuisines: Tobacco Shop, Bar
Average price: Expensive
Area: Upper East Side
Address: 26 E 63rd St
New York, NY 10021
Phone: (212) 752-8200

#315
718 Hookah Lounge & Grill
Cuisines: Hookah Bar, Lounge, Mediterranean
Average price: Modest
Area: Forest Hills
Address: 72-13 Austin St
Forest Hills, NY 11375
Phone: (718) 520-7213

#316
The Daily
Cuisines: Bar
Average price: Modest
Area: Nolita
Address: 210 Elizabeth St
New York, NY 10012
Phone: (212) 343-7011

#317
Divine Bar & Grill
Cuisines: Bar, Pool Hall, American
Average price: Modest
Area: Bedford Stuyvesant, Bushwick
Address: 896 Broadway
Brooklyn, NY 11206
Phone: (718) 455-5455

#318
Bluebird Food & Spirits
Cuisines: American, Bar
Average price: Modest
Area: Prospect Lefferts Gardens
Address: 504 Flatbush Ave
Brooklyn, NY 11225
Phone: (718) 484-9494

#319
Jack's Fire Dept
Cuisines: Pub, Sports Bar
Average price: Inexpensive
Area: Sunnyside
Address: 39-46 Skillman Ave
Sunnyside, NY 11104
Phone: (718) 784-9090

#320
Upholstery Store: Food & Wine
Cuisines: Wine Bar
Average price: Modest
Area: West Village
Address: 713 Washington St
New York, NY 10014
Phone: (212) 352-2300

#321
The Campbell Terrace
Cuisines: Lounge
Average price: Expensive
Area: Midtown East
Address: 15 Vanderbilt Ave
New York, NY 10017
Phone: (212) 953-0409

#322
Cielo At the Mayfair
Cuisines: Italian, Bar
Average price: Modest
Area: Midtown West, Theater District
Address: 242 W 49th St
New York, NY 10019
Phone: (212) 489-8600

#323
Bedlam
Cuisines: Night Club, Lounge
Average price: Modest
Area: East Village, Alphabet City
Address: 40 Ave C
New York, NY 10009
Phone: (212) 228-1049

#324
The Place Bar and Lounge
Cuisines: Burgers, Pizza, Sports Bar
Average price: Modest
Area: Greenpoint
Address: 269 Norman Ave
Brooklyn, NY 11222
Phone: (718) 383-1900

#325
The Jar
Cuisines: Dive Bar, Beer Garden, Pub
Average price: Inexpensive
Area: Sunnyside
Address: 4506 48th Ave
Woodside, NY 11377
Phone: (718) 784-9616

#326
Nostrand Avenue Pub
Cuisines: Bar
Average price: Inexpensive
Area: Crown Heights
Address: 658 Nostrand Ave
Brooklyn, NY 11216
Phone: (718) 483-9699

#327
Union Grounds
Cuisines: Comfort Food, Sports Bar
Average price: Modest
Area: Carroll Gardens, Gowanus
Address: 270 Smith St
New York, NY 11231
Phone: (347) 763-1935

#328
Acey Ducey's
Cuisines: Pub
Average price: Modest
Area: Forest Hills
Address: 101-17 Metropolitan Ave
Forest Hills, NY 11375
Phone: (718) 575-5055

#329
SoHo Cigar Bar
Cuisines: Cocktail Bar, Vape Shop
Average price: Modest
Area: South Village
Address: 32 Watts St
New York, NY 10013
Phone: (212) 941-1781

#330
Post Office
Cuisines: Bar, American
Average price: Modest
Area: Williamsburg - South Side
Address: 188 Havemeyer St
Brooklyn, NY 11211
Phone: (718) 963-2574

#331
Dominion NY Theater & Lounge
Cuisines: Music Venues, Lounge
Average price: Inexpensive
Area: NoHo
Address: 428 Lafayette St
Manhattan, NY 10003
Phone: (888) 882-1951

#332
Church Publick
Cuisines: American, Pub
Average price: Modest
Area: Civic Center, TriBeCa
Address: 82 Reade St
New York, NY 10007
Phone: (212) 267-3000

#333
Triona's
Cuisines: Sports Bar, Irish Pub
Average price: Inexpensive
Area: Greenwich Village
Address: 237 Sullivan St
New York, NY 10012
Phone: (212) 982-5222

#334
Ore Bar
Cuisines: Bar
Average price: Modest
Area: Williamsburg - North Side
Address: 277 Graham Avenue
Brooklyn, NY 11211
Phone: (718) 387-2541

#335
The Baroness Bar
Cuisines: Wine Bar, Champagne Bar
Average price: Modest
Area: Long Island City
Address: 41-26 Crescent St
Long Island City, NY 11101
Phone: (718) 784-5065

#336
Draught 55
Cuisines: Bar
Average price: Modest
Area: Midtown East
Address: 245 E 55th St
New York, NY 10022
Phone: (212) 300-4096

#337
Bungalo Lounge
Cuisines: Lounge
Average price: Modest
Area: Astoria
Address: 32-03 Broadway
Astoria, NY 11106
Phone: (718) 204-7010

#338
Perdition NYC
Cuisines: Pub
Average price: Modest
Area: Hell's Kitchen, Midtown West
Address: 692 10th Ave
New York, NY 10019
Phone: (212) 582-5660

#339
St Gambrinus Beer Shoppe
Cuisines: Bar, Beer, Wine, Spirits
Average price: Modest
Area: Boerum Hill
Address: 533 Atlantic Ave
Brooklyn, NY 11217
Phone: (347) 763-2261

#340
The Whiskey Rebel
Cuisines: Pub, Sports Bar
Average price: Modest
Area: Kips Bay, Flatiron
Address: 129 Lexington Ave
New York, NY 10016
Phone: (212) 686-3800

#341
The Crown Inn
Cuisines: Bar
Average price: Modest
Area: Crown Heights
Address: 724 Franklin Ave
Brooklyn, NY 11238
Phone: (347) 915-1131

#342
Rose Club, Champagne Bar
Cuisines: Champagne Bar
Average price: Exclusive
Area: Midtown West, Midtown East
Address: 768 5th Ave
New York, NY 10019
Phone: (212) 759-3000

#343
On The Rocks
Cuisines: Lounge
Average price: Modest
Area: Hell's Kitchen, Midtown West
Address: 696 10th Ave
New York, NY 10019
Phone: (212) 247-2055

#344
State Grill and Bar
Cuisines: Bar, American
Average price: Expensive
Area: Midtown West, Koreatown
Address: 350 5th Ave
Manhattan, NY 10016
Phone: (212) 216-9693

#345
RockBar
Cuisines: Gay Bar
Average price: Inexpensive
Area: West Village
Address: 185 Christopher St
Manhattan, NY 10014
Phone: (212) 675-1864

#346
The Bodega
Cuisines: Pub, Breakfast & Brunch
Average price: Modest
Area: Bushwick
Address: 24 St. Nicholas Ave
Brooklyn, NY 11237
Phone: (347) 305-3344

#347
Viva Toro
Cuisines: Bar, Mexican, Latin American
Average price: Modest
Area: Williamsburg - North Side
Address: 188 Berry St
Brooklyn, NY 11249
Phone: (718) 384-2138

#348
D Bar
Cuisines: Wine Bar, Cocktail Bar
Average price: Exclusive
Area: Chelsea
Address: 263 W 19th St
New York, NY 10011
Phone: (212) 493-5150

#349
Bemelmans Bar
Cuisines: Lounge
Average price: Exclusive
Area: Upper East Side
Address: 35 E 76th St
New York, NY 10021
Phone: (212) 744-1600

#350
Bembe
Cuisines: Night Club
Average price: Modest
Area: Williamsburg - South Side, South Williamsburg
Address: 81 S 6th St
Brooklyn, NY 11211
Phone: (718) 387-5389

#351
Blue Ribbon Downing Street Bar
Cuisines: Lounge
Average price: Expensive
Area: West Village
Address: 34 Downing St
New York, NY 10014
Phone: (212) 691-0404

#352
Whiskey Soda Lounge NY
Cuisines: Bar, Thai
Average price: Modest
Area: Columbia Street Waterfront District
Address: 115 Columbia St
Brooklyn, NY 11201
Phone: (718) 797-4120

#353
Adelina's
Cuisines: Italian, Wine Bar, Pizza
Average price: Modest
Area: Greenpoint
Address: 159 Greenpoint Ave
Brooklyn, NY 11222
Phone: (347) 763-0152

#354
Midway Bar
Cuisines: Bar
Average price: Inexpensive
Area: Williamsburg - South Side
Address: 272 Grand St
Brooklyn, NY 11211
Phone: (718) 599-1969

#355
The Bar Room
Cuisines: Restaurant, Bar
Average price: Modest
Area: Upper East Side
Address: 117 E 60th St
New York, NY 10022
Phone: (212) 561-5523

#356
Ryan Maguire's Ale House
Cuisines: Pub, American, Irish
Average price: Modest
Area: Financial District
Address: 28 Cliff St
New York, NY 10038
Phone: (212) 566-6906

#357
Cotenna
Cuisines: Wine Bar, Italian
Average price: Modest
Area: West Village
Address: 21 Bedford St
New York, NY 10014
Phone: (646) 861-0175

#358
The Tippler
Cuisines: Bar
Average price: Modest
Area: Chelsea, Meatpacking District
Address: 425 W 15th St
New York, NY 10011
Phone: (212) 206-0000

#359
Injera
Cuisines: Ethiopian, Bar
Average price: Modest
Area: West Village
Address: 11 Abingdon Sq
New York, NY 10014
Phone: (212) 206-9330

#360
Havana Dreams
Cuisines: Lounge, Tobacco Shop
Average price: Modest
Area: Middle Village
Address: 63-10 Woodhaven Blvd
Middle Village, NY 11367
Phone: (718) 685-0078

#361
TØRST
Cuisines: Pub
Average price: Modest
Area: Greenpoint
Address: 615 Manhattan Ave
Brooklyn, NY 11222
Phone: (718) 389-6034

#362
The Headless Horseman
Cuisines: Bar
Average price: Modest
Area: Union Square, Gramercy, Flatiron
Address: 119 E 15th St
New York, NY 10003
Phone: (212) 777-5101

#363
Sharlene's
Cuisines: Bar
Average price: Inexpensive
Area: Prospect Heights
Address: 353 Flatbush Ave
Brooklyn, NY 11238
Phone: (718) 638-1272

#364
Boat Bar
Cuisines: Dive Bar
Average price: Inexpensive
Area: Cobble Hill, Boerum Hill
Address: 175 Smith St
Brooklyn, NY 11201
Phone: (718) 254-0607

#365
Hibernia
Cuisines: Bar, American
Average price: Modest
Area: Hell's Kitchen, Midtown West
Address: 401 W 50th St
New York, NY 10019
Phone: (212) 969-9703

#366
Pearl's Social & Billy Club
Cuisines: Dive Bar, Cocktail Bar
Average price: Modest
Area: Bushwick
Address: 40 Saint Nicholas Ave
Brooklyn, NY 11237
Phone: (347) 627-9985

#367
The Pop Bar
Cuisines: Cocktail Bar
Average price: Inexpensive
Area: Astoria
Address: 12-21 Astoria Blvd
Astoria, NY 11102
Phone: (718) 204-8313

#368
Living Room Restaurant & Lounge
Cuisines: American, Lounge
Average price: Modest
Area: Gravesend
Address: 178 Ave U
Brooklyn, NY 11223
Phone: (718) 996-8700

#369
McMahon's Public House
Cuisines: Sports Bar, Irish
Average price: Modest
Area: Park Slope
Address: 39 5th Ave
Brooklyn, NY 11217
Phone: (718) 230-4549

#370
Aldo Sohm Wine Bar
Cuisines: Wine Bar, French, American
Average price: Expensive
Area: Midtown West, Theater District
Address: 151 W 51st St
New York, NY 10019
Phone: (212) 554-1143

#371
Antler Beer And Wine Dispensary
Cuisines: Wine Bar
Average price: Modest
Area: Lower East Side
Address: 123 Allen St
New York, NY 10002
Phone: (212) 432-5000

#372
Whiskey Blue
Cuisines: Lounge
Average price: Expensive
Area: Midtown East
Address: 541 Lexington Ave
New York, NY 10022
Phone: (212) 407-2947

#373
Spur Tree
Cuisines: Caribbean, Lounge, Asian Fusion
Average price: Modest
Area: Lower East Side
Address: 74 Orchard St
New York, NY 10002
Phone: (646) 481-1229

#374
The Abbey Bar
Cuisines: Dive Bar, Beer, Wine, Spirits, Cocktail Bar
Average price: Inexpensive
Area: Williamsburg - North Side
Address: 536 Driggs Ave
Brooklyn, NY 11211
Phone: (718) 599-4400

#375
Alaska
Cuisines: Bar
Average price: Inexpensive
Area: East Williamsburg
Address: 35 Ingraham St
Brooklyn, NY 11206
Phone: (718) 628-3643

#376
Session House
Cuisines: Irish, Pub
Average price: Modest
Area: Midtown East
Address: 1009 2nd Ave
New York, NY 10022
Phone: (646) 559-4404

#377
The Storehouse
Cuisines: Pub
Average price: Modest
Area: Flatiron
Address: 69 W 23rd St
Manhattan, NY 10010
Phone: (212) 243-8898

#378
Bar Chord
Cuisines: Bar
Average price: Modest
Area: Flatbush
Address: 1008 Cortelyou Rd
Brooklyn, NY 11210
Phone: (347) 240-6033

#379
The Narrows
Cuisines: Bar, American
Average price: Modest
Area: East Williamsburg, Bushwick
Address: 1037 Flushing Ave
Brooklyn, NY 11237
Phone: (281) 827-1800

#380
Beer Culture
Cuisines: Beer, Wine, Spirits, Bar
Average price: Modest
Area: Hell's Kitchen, Midtown West, Theater District
Address: 328 W 45th St
New York, NY 10036
Phone: (646) 590-2139

#381
At Nine Restaurant & Bar
Cuisines: Thai, Cocktail Bar
Average price: Modest
Area: Hell's Kitchen, Midtown West, Theater District
Address: 592 9th Ave
New York, NY 10036
Phone: (212) 265-4499

#382
Bar 54
Cuisines: Cocktail Bar
Average price: Expensive
Area: Midtown West, Theater District
Address: 135 W 45th St
New York, NY 10036
Phone: (646) 364-1234

#383
Eve's Lounge
Cuisines: Lounge
Average price: Modest
Area: Crown Heights, Prospect Heights
Address: 769 Washington Ave
Brooklyn, NY 11238
Phone: (347) 442-5959

#384
Manhattan Proper
Cuisines: Sports Bar, American, Lounge
Average price: Modest
Area: Civic Center, TriBeCa
Address: 6 Murray St
New York, NY 10007
Phone: (646) 559-4445

#385
Gabbana
Cuisines: Lounge
Average price: Expensive
Area: North Corona
Address: 107-11 Northern Blvd
Corona, NY 11369
Phone: (718) 651-4052

#386
Pumps Bar
Cuisines: Bar, Adult Entertainment
Average price: Modest
Area: East Williamsburg
Address: 1089 Grand St
Brooklyn, NY 11211
Phone: (718) 599-2474

#387
Pete's Candy Store
Cuisines: Music Venues, Dive Bar, Pub
Average price: Inexpensive
Area: Williamsburg - North Side
Address: 709 Lorimer St
Brooklyn, NY 11211
Phone: (718) 302-3770

#388
Brooklyn Ice House
Cuisines: Barbeque, Pub
Average price: Inexpensive
Area: Red Hook
Address: 318 Van Brunt St
Brooklyn, NY 11231
Phone: (718) 222-1865

#389
The 55 Bar
Cuisines: Jazz, Blues, Bar
Average price: Inexpensive
Area: West Village
Address: 55 Christopher St
New York, NY 10001
Phone: (212) 929-9883

#390
Maru
Cuisines: Lounge, Karaoke, Korean
Average price: Modest
Area: Midtown West, Koreatown
Address: 11 W 32nd St
New York, NY 10001
Phone: (212) 273-3413

#391
Domaine Wine Bar
Cuisines: Wine Bar, Jazz, Blues
Average price: Modest
Area: Hunters Point, Long Island City
Address: 50-04 Vernon Blvd
Long Island City, NY 11101
Phone: (718) 784-2350

#392
Flying Lobster
Cuisines: Wine Bar
Average price: Expensive
Area: Carroll Gardens, Columbia Street Waterfront District
Address: 144 Union St
Brooklyn, NY 11231
Phone: (718) 855-2633

#393
Ara
Cuisines: Wine Bar, Coffee, Tea, Cocktail Bar
Average price: Modest
Area: West Village, Meatpacking District
Address: 24 9th Ave
New York, NY 10014
Phone: (212) 255-5588

#394
David Burke Garden & Treehouse Bar
Cuisines: Bar, American
Average price: Expensive
Area: South Village
Address: 23 Grand St
New York, NY 10013
Phone: (212) 201-9119

#395
Bondurants
Cuisines: Cocktail Bar, American, Gastropub
Average price: Modest
Area: Yorkville, Upper East Side
Address: 303 E 85th St
New York, NY 10028
Phone: (212) 249-1509

#396
The Duck
Cuisines: Dive Bar
Average price: Inexpensive
Area: East Harlem
Address: 2171 2nd Ave
New York, NY 10029
Phone: (212) 831-0000

#397
Turks & Frogs
Cuisines: Wine Bar, Turkish
Average price: Modest
Area: West Village
Address: 323 W 11th St #2
New York, NY 10014
Phone: (212) 691-8875

#398
Simone Martini Bar Cafe
Cuisines: Lounge, American, Cocktail Bar
Average price: Modest
Area: East Village
Address: 134 1st Ave
New York, NY 10009
Phone: (212) 982-6665

#399
One Mile House
Cuisines: Bar, American
Average price: Modest
Area: Lower East Side
Address: 10 Delancey St
New York, NY 10002
Phone: (646) 559-0702

#400
Pencil Factory Bar
Cuisines: Bar
Average price: Inexpensive
Area: Greenpoint
Address: 142 Franklin St
Brooklyn, NY 11222
Phone: (718) 609-5858

#401
The Pony Bar
Cuisines: Bar
Average price: Modest
Area: Yorkville, Upper East Side
Address: 1444 1st Ave
New York, NY 10021
Phone: (212) 288-0090

#402
Billymark's West
Cuisines: Dive Bar
Average price: Inexpensive
Area: Chelsea, Midtown West
Address: 332 9th Ave
New York, NY 10001
Phone: (212) 629-0118

#403
KRUSH
Cuisines: Sports Bar, Korean, Asian Fusion
Average price: Modest
Area: Midtown West, Koreatown
Address: 2 W 32nd St
New York, NY 10001
Phone: (917) 864-9456

#404
Rocks Off Concert Cruise
Cuisines: Bar, Music Venues
Average price: Inexpensive
Area: Kips Bay, Stuyvesant Town
Address: 2430 FDR Dr
New York, NY 10010
Phone: (917) 524-8666

#405
Big Bar
Cuisines: Bar
Average price: Modest
Area: East Village
Address: 75 E 7th St
New York, NY 10003
Phone: (212) 777-6969

#406
Good Co.
Cuisines: Bar
Average price: Inexpensive
Area: Williamsburg - North Side
Address: 10 Hope St
Brooklyn, NY 11211
Phone: (718) 218-7191

#407
Puffy's Tavern
Cuisines: Bar
Average price: Modest
Area: TriBeCa
Address: 81 Hudson St
New York, NY 10013
Phone: (212) 227-3912

#408
Harding's
Cuisines: American, Cocktail Bar
Average price: Modest
Area: Flatiron
Address: 32 E 21st St
New York, NY 10010
Phone: (212) 600-2105

#409
Maggie Reilly's
Cuisines: Pub
Average price: Modest
Area: Chelsea, Midtown West
Address: 340 9th Ave
New York, NY 10001
Phone: (646) 476-3209

#410
Dram
Cuisines: Cocktail Bar
Average price: Modest
Area: Williamsburg - South Side
Address: 177 S 4th St
Brooklyn, NY 11211
Phone: (718) 486-3726

#411
Bailey's Corner Pub
Cuisines: Pub
Average price: Inexpensive
Area: Yorkville, Upper East Side
Address: 1607 York Ave
New York, NY 10028
Phone: (212) 650-1341

#412
Entwine
Cuisines: Bar
Average price: Modest
Area: West Village
Address: 765 Washington St
New York, NY 10014
Phone: (212) 727-8765

#413
Bill's Place
Cuisines: Jazz, Blues
Average price: Inexpensive
Area: Harlem
Address: 148 W 133rd St
New York, NY 10030
Phone: (212) 281-0777

#414
Kinfolk
Cuisines: Coffee, Tea, Lounge
Average price: Modest
Area: Williamsburg - North Side
Address: 90 Wythe Ave
Brooklyn, NY 11249
Phone: (347) 799-2946

#415
The Cricketers Arms
Cuisines: British, Pub, Sports Bar
Average price: Modest
Area: TriBeCa
Address: 57 Murray St
New York, NY 10007
Phone: (212) 619-5550

#416
Cello Wine Bar
Cuisines: Wine Bar
Average price: Modest
Area: Midtown East
Address: 229 E 53rd St
New York, NY 10022
Phone: (917) 475-1131

#417
Marshall Stack
Cuisines: Bar
Average price: Modest
Area: Lower East Side
Address: 66 Rivington St
New York, NY 10002
Phone: (212) 228-4667

#418
Station Cafe
Cuisines: Dive Bar
Average price: Inexpensive
Area: Woodside
Address: 39-50 61st St
Woodside, NY 11377
Phone: (718) 429-9464

#419
South 4th Bar & Café
Cuisines: Coffee, Tea, Bar
Average price: Inexpensive
Area: Williamsburg - South Side
Address: 90 S 4th St
Brooklyn, NY 11249
Phone: (718) 218-7478

#420
RARE View Rooftop
Cuisines: Cocktail Bar,
Breakfast & Brunch, Burgers
Average price: Modest
Area: Midtown East, Murray Hill
Address: 303 Lexington Ave
New York, NY 10016
Phone: (212) 481-1999

#421
Center Bar
Cuisines: American, Lounge
Average price: Expensive
Area: Hell's Kitchen, Midtown West
Address: 10 Columbus Cir
New York, NY 10019
Phone: (212) 823-9500

#422
La Bodega 47 Social Club
Cuisines: Latin American, Cocktail Bar
Average price: Modest
Area: Harlem
Address: 161 Lenox Ave
Manhattan, NY 10026
Phone: (212) 280-4700

#423
FC Gotham
Cuisines: Sports Bar, American, Lounge
Average price: Modest
Area: West Village, Meatpacking District
Address: 409 W 13th St
Manhattan, NY 10014
Phone: (212) 255-5344

#424
The Adirondack
Cuisines: Bar
Average price: Modest
Area: Windsor Terrace
Address: 1241A Prospect Ave
Brooklyn, NY 11218
Phone: (718) 871-0100

#425
The Paper Box
Cuisines: Bar, Music Venues, Venues, Event Space
Average price: Modest
Area: East Williamsburg
Address: 17 Meadow St
Brooklyn, NY 11206
Phone: (718) 383-3815

#426
Barcade
Cuisines: Sports Bar, Burgers, Sandwiches
Average price: Modest
Area: Chelsea
Address: 148 W 24th St
New York, NY 10011
Phone: (212) 390-8455

#427
Pickle Shack
Cuisines: Bar, Vegetarian, Sandwiches
Average price: Modest
Area: Park Slope, Gowanus
Address: 256 4th Ave
New York, NY 11215
Phone: (347) 763-2127

#428
Bubble Lounge
Cuisines: Lounge
Average price: Expensive
Area: TriBeCa
Address: 228 West Broadway #1
New York, NY 10013
Phone: (212) 431-3433

#429
Clem's
Cuisines: Bar
Average price: Inexpensive
Area: Williamsburg - South Side
Address: 264 Grand St
Brooklyn, NY 11211
Phone: (718) 387-9617

#430
Delta Sky Lounge
Cuisines: Lounge
Average price: Modest
Area: LaGuardia Airport
Address: Laguardia Airport
Elmhurst, NY 11369
Phone: (214) 295-3171

#431
Vodou Bar
Cuisines: Bar
Average price: Modest
Area: Bedford Stuyvesant
Address: 95 Halsey St
Brooklyn, NY 11216
Phone: (347) 405-7011

#432
Three of Cups Lounge
Cuisines: Lounge
Average price: Inexpensive
Area: East Village
Address: 83 1st Ave
New York, NY 10003
Phone: (212) 388-0059

#433
L.I.C. Bar
Cuisines: Bar, Music Venues
Average price: Modest
Area: Hunters Point, Long Island City
Address: 4558 Vernon Blvd
Long Island City, NY 11101
Phone: (646) 979-9878

#434
Joe & MissesDoe
Cuisines: American, Bar
Average price: Modest
Area: East Village
Address: 45 E 1st St
New York, NY 10003
Phone: (212) 780-0262

#435
Barramundi
Cuisines: Lounge, Pub, Cocktail Bar
Average price: Inexpensive
Area: Lower East Side
Address: 67 Clinton St
New York, NY 10002
Phone: (212) 529-6999

#436
Cork 'n Fork
Cuisines: Tapas, Wine Bar
Average price: Modest
Area: East Village, Alphabet City
Address: 186 Ave A
New York, NY 10009
Phone: (646) 707-0707

#437
Broadway Dive Bar
Cuisines: Dive Bar
Average price: Inexpensive
Area: Manhattan Valley
Address: 2662 Broadway
New York, NY 10025
Phone: (212) 865-2662

#438
Jasper's Taphouse + Kitchen
Cuisines: American, Pub
Average price: Modest
Area: Hell's Kitchen, Midtown West, Theater District
Address: 761 9th Ave
New York, NY 10019
Phone: (212) 957-1000

#439
Toad Hall
Cuisines: Pub, American
Average price: Modest
Area: SoHo, TriBeCa
Address: 57 Grand St
New York, NY 10013
Phone: (212) 431-8145

#440
Issue Project Room
Cuisines: Performing Arts, Music Venues
Average price: Inexpensive
Area: Brooklyn Heights, Downtown Brooklyn
Address: 22 Boerum Pl
Brooklyn, NY 11201
Phone: (718) 330-0313

#441
The Garret
Cuisines: Bar
Average price: Modest
Area: West Village
Address: 296 Bleecker St
New York, NY 10014
Phone: (212) 675-6157

#442
The Butterfly
Cuisines: Cocktail Bar, American
Average price: Modest
Area: TriBeCa
Address: 225 W Broadway
New York, NY 10013
Phone: (646) 692-4943

#443
Roebling Inn
Cuisines: Pub
Average price: Inexpensive
Area: Brooklyn Heights
Address: 97 Atlantic Ave
Brooklyn, NY 11201
Phone: (718) 488-0040

#444
Cuckoo's Nest
Cuisines: Irish, Pub
Average price: Modest
Area: Woodside
Address: 6104 Woodside Ave
Woodside, NY 11377
Phone: (718) 426-5684

#445
Parkside Lounge
Cuisines: Music Venues, Lounge
Average price: Inexpensive
Area: Lower East Side
Address: 317 E Houston St
New York, NY 10002
Phone: (212) 673-6270

#446
LIC Landing by Coffeed
Cuisines: Venues, Event Space, Coffee, Tea, Bar
Average price: Modest
Area: Hunters Point
Address: 52-10 Center Blvd
Long Island City, NY 11101
Phone: (347) 706-4696

#447
District M
Cuisines: Breakfast & Brunch, Cocktail Bar, Music Venues
Average price: Modest
Area: Midtown West, Theater District
Address: 700 8th Ave
New York, NY 10036
Phone: (212) 869-3600

#448
Saleya
Cuisines: American, Mediterranean, Bar
Average price: Modest
Area: TriBeCa
Address: 65 W Broadway
New York, NY 10007
Phone: (212) 510-7390

#449
Kent Ale House
Cuisines: Bar
Average price: Modest
Area: Williamsburg - North Side
Address: 51 Kent Ave
Brooklyn, NY 11249
Phone: (347) 227-8624

#450
Dublin House
Cuisines: Pub, Dive Bar
Average price: Modest
Area: Upper West Side
Address: 225 W 79th St
New York, NY 10024
Phone: (212) 874-9528

#451
Orient Express Cocktail Bar
Cuisines: Bar, Mediterranean
Average price: Modest
Area: West Village
Address: 325 West 11th Street
New York, NY 10014
Phone: (212) 691-8845

#452
The Upstairs Pub
Cuisines: Pub
Average price: Inexpensive
Area: Midtown East, Murray Hill
Address: 369 Lexington Ave
Manhattan, NY 10017
Phone: (212) 986-0500

#453
Bushwick Country Club
Cuisines: Bar, Mini Golf
Average price: Inexpensive
Area: East Williamsburg
Address: 618 Grand St
Brooklyn, NY 11211
Phone: (718) 388-2114

#454
Drunken Monkey Bar & Grill
Cuisines: Bar, American
Average price: Modest
Area: Westerleigh
Address: 1205 Forest Ave
Staten Island, NY 10310
Phone: (718) 273-2267

#455
Tom & Jerry's
Cuisines: Bar
Average price: Modest
Area: NoHo
Address: 288 Elizabeth St
New York, NY 10012
Phone: (212) 260-5045

#456
Grand Ferry Tavern
Cuisines: Cocktail Bar, Seafood, American
Average price: Modest
Area: Williamsburg - North Side
Address: 229 Kent Ave
Brooklyn, NY 11249
Phone: (718) 782-8500

#457
Washington Commons
Cuisines: Pub
Average price: Inexpensive
Area: Crown Heights, Prospect Heights
Address: 748 Washington Ave
Brooklyn, NY 11238
Phone: (718) 230-3666

#458
The Ides Bar
Cuisines: Bar
Average price: Modest
Area: Williamsburg - North Side
Address: 80 Wythe Ave
Brooklyn, NY 11249
Phone: (718) 460-8006

#459
Kingside
Cuisines: Cocktail Bar, American
Average price: Expensive
Area: Midtown West
Address: 124 W 57th St
New York, NY 10019
Phone: (212) 707-8000

#460
Urbo NYC
Cuisines: American, Cocktail Bar
Average price: Modest
Area: Midtown West, Theater District
Address: 11 Times Sq
Manhattan, NY 10036
Phone: (212) 542-8950

#461
Decoy
Cuisines: Dim Sum, Bar
Average price: Expensive
Area: West Village
Address: 529 Hudson St
New York, NY 10014
Phone: (212) 691-9700

#462
The Junction
Cuisines: Sports Bar, Pub, Burgers
Average price: Modest
Area: Midtown East, Murray Hill
Address: 329 Lexington Ave
New York, NY 10016
Phone: (212) 682-7700

#463
Beacon Bar
Cuisines: Cocktail Bar
Average price: Modest
Area: Upper West Side
Address: 2130 Broadway 75th St
Manhattan, NY 10023
Phone: (212) 787-1100

#464
Living Room Bar
Cuisines: Lounge, Cocktail Bar
Average price: Expensive
Area: Financial District
Address: 123 Washington St
New York, NY 10006
Phone: (646) 826-8642

#465
Bar Basso
Cuisines: Italian, Bar
Average price: Modest
Area: Midtown West
Address: 235 W 56 St
New York, NY 10019
Phone: (212) 510-8356

#466
Metropolitan Club
Cuisines: Nightlife
Average price: Exclusive
Area: Upper East Side
Address: 1 E 60th St
New York, NY 10022
Phone: (212) 838-7400

#467
The Hangar Bar
Cuisines: Gay Bar, Wine Bar, Lounge
Average price: Inexpensive
Area: West Village
Address: 115 Christopher St
New York, NY 10014
Phone: (212) 627-2044

#468
Casa Lounge
Cuisines: Hookah Bar, Moroccan
Average price: Inexpensive
Area: Astoria
Address: 2557 Steinway St
Astoria, NY 11103
Phone: (347) 639-0954

#469
SubCulture
Cuisines: Music Venues
Average price: Modest
Area: NoHo
Address: 45 Bleecker St
New York, NY 10012
Phone: (212) 533-5470

#470
O'hanlons
Cuisines: Sports Bar, Pool Hall
Average price: Inexpensive
Area: Stuyvesant Town, Gramercy, East Village
Address: 349 E 14th St
New York, NY 10003
Phone: (212) 533-7333

#471
Dining Room
Cuisines: American, Bar
Average price: Modest
Area: Downtown Brooklyn
Address: 56 Willoughby St
Brooklyn, NY 11201
Phone: (718) 488-8902

#472
La Piscine
Cuisines: Bar, Mediterranean
Average price: Expensive
Area: Chelsea
Address: 518 W 27th St
New York, NY 10001
Phone: (212) 525-0000

#473
Shenanigans Pub
Cuisines: Karaoke, Music Venues, Irish Pub
Average price: Inexpensive
Area: Kensington, Flatbush
Address: 802 Caton Ave
Brooklyn, NY 11218
Phone: (718) 633-3689

#474
Larry Lawrence
Cuisines: Lounge
Average price: Modest
Area: Williamsburg - South Side, Williamsburg - North Side
Address: 295 Grand St
Brooklyn, NY 11211
Phone: (718) 218-7866

#475
Night of Joy
Cuisines: Lounge
Average price: Modest
Area: Williamsburg - North Side
Address: 667 Lorimer St
Brooklyn, NY 11211
Phone: (718) 388-8693

#476
The Runner
Cuisines: American, Bar, American
Average price: Modest
Area: Clinton Hill
Address: 458 Myrtle Ave
New York, NY 11205
Phone: (718) 643-6500

#477
The Madison Room
Cuisines: Bar, American
Average price: Exclusive
Area: Midtown East
Address: 455 Madison Ave
New York, NY 10022
Phone: (212) 891-8100

#478
Bar Reis
Cuisines: Bar
Average price: Inexpensive
Area: Park Slope
Address: 375 5th Ave
Brooklyn, NY 11215
Phone: (718) 974-2412

#479
Scratcher
Cuisines: Pub, American
Average price: Inexpensive
Area: East Village
Address: 209 E 5th St
New York, NY 10003
Phone: (212) 477-0030

#480
Floyd, NY
Cuisines: Bar
Average price: Inexpensive
Area: Brooklyn Heights
Address: 131 Atlantic Ave
Brooklyn, NY 11201
Phone: (718) 858-5810

#481
Tribeca Tap House
Cuisines: Sports Bar, Gastropub, Burgers
Average price: Modest
Area: TriBeCa
Address: 363 Greenwich St
New York, NY 10013
Phone: (212) 510-8939

#482
The Rum House
Cuisines: Lounge, Cocktail Bar
Average price: Modest
Area: Midtown West, Theater District
Address: 228 W 47th St
New York, NY 10036
Phone: (646) 490-6924

#483
Gotham Lounge
Cuisines: American, Lounge
Average price: Expensive
Area: Midtown West
Address: 700 5th Ave
Manhattan, NY 10019
Phone: (212) 956-2888

#484
Uvarara
Cuisines: Italian, Wine Bar
Average price: Expensive
Area: Middle Village
Address: 79-28 Metropolitan Ave
Middle Village, NY 11379
Phone: (718) 894-0052

#485
Characters NYC
Cuisines: Bar
Average price: Modest
Area: Midtown West, Theater District
Address: 245 W 54th St
New York, NY 10019
Phone: (212) 459-8904

#486
Blew Smoke Cigar Room
Cuisines: Tobacco Shop, Lounge
Average price: Modest
Area: Crown Heights, Prospect Heights
Address: 593 Washington Ave
Brooklyn, NY 11238
Phone: (718) 789-7665

#487
Arthur Murray Dance Studio
Cuisines: Night Club, Dance School, Dance Studio
Average price: Expensive
Area: Midtown West, Koreatown
Address: 286 5th Ave
New York, NY 10001
Phone: (212) 473-2623

#488
Rose Bar
Cuisines: Lounge
Average price: Exclusive
Area: Gramercy, Flatiron
Address: 2 Lexington Ave
New York, NY 10010
Phone: (212) 920-3300

#489
Fat Buddha
Cuisines: Bar, Asian Fusion, Korean
Average price: Modest
Area: East Village, Alphabet City
Address: 212 Ave A
New York, NY 10009
Phone: (212) 598-0500

#490
Peter Dillon's
Cuisines: Pub
Average price: Inexpensive
Area: Midtown East, Murray Hill
Address: 130 E 40th St
New York, NY 10016
Phone: (212) 213-3998

#491
Vin Sur Vingt
Cuisines: Wine Bar, French
Average price: Expensive
Area: West Village
Address: 201 W 11th St
New York, NY 10014
Phone: (212) 924-4442

#492
Bar-Tini Ultra Lounge
Cuisines: Lounge, Gay Bar
Average price: Modest
Area: Hell's Kitchen, Midtown West
Address: 642 10th Ave
New York, NY 10036
Phone: (917) 388-2897

#493
Brooklyn Fire Proof East
Cuisines: Bar, Café
Average price: Inexpensive
Area: East Williamsburg, Bushwick
Address: 119 Ingraham St
Brooklyn, NY 11237
Phone: (347) 223-4211

#494
LP & Harmony
Cuisines: Bar
Average price: Inexpensive
Area: Williamsburg - North Side
Address: 683 Grand St
Brooklyn, NY 11211
Phone: (347) 262-4274

#495
Lovers of Today
Cuisines: Lounge
Average price: Modest
Area: East Village, Alphabet City
Address: 132 1/2 E 7th St
New York, NY 10009
Phone: (212) 420-9517

#496
Linen Hall
Cuisines: Bar, American
Average price: Modest
Area: East Village
Address: 101 3rd Ave
New York, NY 10003
Phone: (646) 602-9316

#497
Don Pedro
Cuisines: Music Venues, Bar, Mexican
Average price: Inexpensive
Area: East Williamsburg
Address: 90 Manhattan Ave
Brooklyn, NY 11206
Phone: (347) 689-3163

#498
2A
Cuisines: Bar
Average price: Inexpensive
Area: East Village, Alphabet City
Address: 25 Ave A
New York, NY 10009
Phone: (212) 505-2466

#499
Parlor
Cuisines: Lounge, Venues, Event Space, American
Average price: Exclusive
Area: South Village
Address: 286 Spring St
Manhattan, NY 10013
Phone: (212) 414-2902

#500
One Last Shag
Cuisines: Bar
Average price: Inexpensive
Area: Bedford Stuyvesant, Clinton Hill
Address: 348 Franklin Ave
Brooklyn, NY 11238
Phone: (718) 398-2472

Printed in Great Britain
by Amazon